D0504802

Penguin Books Ltd, Harmondsworth,
Middlesex, England
Penguin Books, 625 Madison Avenue,
New York, New York 10022, U.S.A.
Penguin Books Australia Ltd, Ringwood,
Victoria, Australia
Penguin Books Canada Ltd, 2801 John Street,
Markham, Ontario, Canada L3R 1B4
Penguin Books (N.Z.) Ltd, 182–190 Wairau Road,
Auckland 10, New Zealand

Fåglar i naturen: Fjäll och skogsland
first published by Wahlström & Widstrand 1978
This translation published 1979

Printed in Portugal by Gris Impressores, Cacém

Filmset in Monophoto Times by
Northumberland Press Ltd,
Gateshead, Tyne and Wear

Contents

Preface

This volume, the fourth in a series of five, describes the European birds that are found in the northern mountain regions outside the Mediterranean countries, the Alps and other high areas in central Europe. Although each volume is designed to be used independently, the reader will find that a combination of any two will be of greater help because they extend the scope of a bird's range. For example, this book, together with *Birds of Sea and Coast*, covers most species occurring in Iceland, the islands of the Atlantic and northern Scandinavia excluding the Arctic coast.

I would like to thank Stellan Hedgren for his valuable assistance in every aspect of the book, and also the other ornithologists who have supplied facts and opinions – especially Håkan Delin and Lars Svensson.

L.J.

Introduction

Our series of five books covers all the bird species breeding and regularly occurring in Europe. Each book discusses a different type of natural environment. This one describes birds breeding in the highland areas of northern Europe, together with those species mainly distributed in the northern conifer zone. It does not include species that breed exclusively in Arctic areas north of the continent of Europe or in tundra close to the sea. Most of these – little stint, knot, sanderling, Brent goose and barnacle goose – occur as migrants along the sea coasts of Europe and have been discussed in *Birds of Sea and Coast*. Nearly all of the species nesting on bare mountains have a wider distribution area in the treeless tundra throughout the Palaearctic. A number of species breeding in the northern conifer zone are also widely distributed elsewhere in Europe, and with a few exceptions all of these have been excluded or described only briefly. Because different biotopes overlap, and because many species occur in more than one biotope, several of the species have also been described in previous volumes. Some of the species portrayed, although in the same plumage, look considerably different when compared with illustrations in earlier volumes. This is because in certain cases I have chosen a slightly different colour, or shown a different degree of feather wear or a different posture to emphasize that the 'look' of a bird may be varied. In other cases the illustration supplements or complements one in a previous volume. This is particularly true, for example, of the black-throated diver in winter dress, bean goose and pink-footed goose, male goosander, female common scoter, adult greenshank, red-necked phalarope (female), the immature broad-billed sandpiper and the adult long-tailed skua in flight. The distribution maps, when compared with previous volumes, reflect these differences.

Readers may note some slight differences in bird measurements between this and previous volumes in the series. A very recent publication, *The Birds of the Western Palaearctic*, Stanley Cramp and K. E. L. Simmons, (eds.), Oxford University Press, 1977, contains much up-to-date material on sizes, ranges, etc. Our data here and in the subsequent volume is based on this new information.

Mountain and forest environments

The birds of northern Europe inhabit an area that includes many types of environments. These types are important because the distribution of animals often coincides to a great extent with the distribution of different plant communities, and plants are the starting point of the food-chains in nature. Within a particular type of environment – a biotope – in a more or less limited area, all the various parts, ranging from micro-organisms to large mammals, interact with one another. Thus, this range of plants and animals forms an ecological system – an ecosystem. The distribution of the plants themselves is determined primarily by climate and soil type.

The conifer zone

The northern hemisphere is encircled by an almost continuous belt of conifers, which in Europe is dominated by pine and spruce. In some areas there are large numbers of deciduous trees, especially aspen, birch, alder and rowan. In Europe the southern boundary of the belt roughly coincides with the 60th parallel; this is the northern boundary of certain hardwood trees – oak and ash, for example – and of many smaller plants. South of this boundary there are patches of conifers inhabited by many of the northern bird species, so the boundary is by no means always an absolute one. Many of the distribution maps reflect this. The hawfinch and the nuthatch are two species whose northern boundary abuts on the conifer zone. But the European conifers also have a *northern* boundary, beyond which other, more cold-resistant, plant communities take over (see section on Mountains). 'Forest zone' is a term applied to the extensive and often flat conifer areas within this conifer zone. 'Taiga' is the name given in this book to the northernmost part of the conifer zone, dominated by spruce with a scattering of birch and a great deal of waterlogged forest and fenland. This region also has abundant bogs, lakes and rivers.

Mountains

The Scandinavian mountain range runs the full length of the Scandinavian peninsula. It has certain characteristics in common with the Arctic tundra and the Arctic areas further north, but it also has a number of specific

Old golden eagle

features. The British Isles, particularly Scotland, also have high mountain areas which share many species with the mountain areas of Fennoscandia, but the climate is more humid and the winters are shorter. There are large areas where the natural vegetation has been cleared and the land is grazed by cattle. Extensive bogs and heaths are typical, and the vegetation belongs to the Atlantic flora. Just as distance from the North Pole affects air temperature and consequently the plant and animal communities, altitude differences have a corresponding and sometimes more pronounced effect. Vegetation zones can be more readily distinguished in the mountains. Spruce, the conifer most resistant to cold, occurs near mountains as a slender tree with short drooping branches to survive the deep snow cover. The mountain birch region, north of the conifer region, often forms dense forests within narrow vertical limits – the birch zone. The 'tree line' is marked by the altitude limit of continuous birch areas, and is defined as the highest altitude at which a tree can live. Above the tree line comes the bare mountain or 'alpine zone'. In other alpine regions, such as the Alps proper or the Atlas mountains, the upper-most stratum of trees may be different, and include other conifers or oak species.

The alpine zone can be divided into low-alpine, intermediate-alpine and high-alpine. Vegetation in the low-alpine zone is often abundant, with occasional birches, osiers, shrubs, berry plants and heathers. The altitude limit of the blueberry marks the beginning of the intermediate-alpine zone, which has a thinner but usually continuous covering of vegetation including, for example, three-leaved rush, least willow, crowberry and Alpine bearberry. The high-alpine zone has only occasional higher plants but often a wealth of lichens. Only the upper part of the Scandinavian mountain range reaches the high-alpine zone. From the tree line and well up into the low-alpine zone, different kinds of willows (woolly willow, bluish willow and least willow) are common and locally predominant (mainly in damper areas); we refer to this region as the 'willow zone'. The bare high-alpine zones are dominated by various lichens – the 'lichen zone'. The height of the various zones above sea-level varies with latitude: the further north, the lower the tree line.

Vegetation is also influenced by other factors, particularly the impact of local topography on the climate. Exposure to cold winds is one factor, and another is that there is more solar irradiation on the south side of a mountain than on the north. Snow is distributed very unevenly on bare mountain, and where there is snow the growth periods are shorter than on boulder ridges, for example. Mountain lakes also affect the local climate. The shore is cooled during spring and summer by the lake water, and if the lake is in a hollow, cold air, which is heavier than warm, descends into it.

Water supply is also a large factor in determining vegetation. In areas where rain or melted snow drains freely through the soil, there is dry, heath-like ground covered with lichen and berry plants. In areas where the bedrock holds the groundwater near the surface, lakes and watercourses are formed. A badly drained area becomes waterlogged and develops into a bog. Mosses and sedges flourish in bogs, and so do osier thickets, which sometimes grow into extensive quagmires. Vegetation is most luxuriant in places where the water flows through the ground surface. Mountain birch areas with abundant vegetation including monk's hood and *Matteuccia struthiopteris* and the osier jungles of mountain slopes are often watered in this way. In summer they look almost tropical and accommodate large numbers of passerines. The nature of the bedrock, especially its lime content, also has a vital bearing on the appearance of the vegetation.

The occurrence of birds in the mountains

There are often very clear links between birds and the different vegetation zones, and the mountain hiker can expect to meet different species at different altitudes. In the forest zone on the continent of Europe there are large areas of inhospitable, often sparse, pine forest with very scattered populations of spotted flycatcher, redstart, perhaps some tree pipits and black woodpeckers. Spruce forest, especially when mixed with hardwood trees, accommodates a wider variety of birds – pine grosbeak, brambling, willow tit, song thrush and Siberian jay. Clear forest lakes provide nesting spots for black-throated diver, goosander, teal, tufted duck and common gull. Most forest owls are found where the continuous forest is interrupted by felled areas, bogs, rivers and open meadows. Waterlogged forest and the edges of bogs are inhabited by rustic and little buntings. Extensive forest marshes are usually the home of several waders, including wood sandpiper, spotted redshank, greenshank, whimbrel, snipe and jack snipe, and broad-billed sandpiper. The short-eared owl and hen harrier will also live there if there is a good supply of small rodents, and passerines will be mainly represented by the meadow pipit. If the marshland has plenty of osiers, grassy meadows and small lakes, the birdwatcher will also see several ducks such as wigeon and mallard, yellow wagtail and whinchat. In the uppermost part of the conifer zone towards the mountain birch region there is the three-toed woodpecker, Siberian tit, brambling and dunnock. Willow warbler, redwing, fieldfare, song thrush, brambling, pied fly-catcher, redpoll and – in damp places – the bluethroat are characteristic residents of mountain birch forest. Above the tree line in the low-alpine zone, with marshes, osier thickets and mountain heaths with scattered birches, there are Lapland bunting, bluethroat and reed bunting.

In marshes and on lakesides you will see the yellow wagtail again, perhaps also red-throated pipit, Temminck's stint, wood sandpiper and, in marshy ponds, the red-necked phalarope. The lakes in this region often support teal, pintail, scaup, common scoter, red-breasted merganser and common gull. Merlins may frequently be observed near the tree line or just above it, and a rough-legged buzzard may appear above a precipice on the bare mountain. The steep slopes left by landslips may be used as breeding grounds by ring ouzels, ravens or the rare gyr falcon. The red-throated diver, long-tailed duck and redshank breed near water above the tree line. The dunlin and the ruff belong in the far-flung sedge marshes well above the tree line. In higher, treeless, mountain heaths there are long-tailed skuas, dotterels, golden plovers, meadow pipits, wheatears and perhaps snowy owls, while gravel ridges are populated by shore larks and ringed plovers. Ptarmigan, snow bunting and purple sandpiper are the only species seen among the boulders of the lava region. Although some species may be scarce, or absent, this picture would be similar in the Highlands of Scotland.

Mountain ecology: a sensitive mechanism

Like other areas with extreme conditions, or rather an alternating variety of very different conditions, the mountains have a delicate equilibrium. Because few animal and plant species have been able to adjust to such an environment, there are often greater numbers of individuals. If there are only a few links in an ecosystem, minor changes will be enough to make considerable disruptions in its equilibrium. The numbers of different bird species in the mountains often fluctuate quite considerably, and these fluctuations are bound up with corresponding variations in other factors. Species with a specialized diet are more sensitive to environmental changes than species which can draw on a wide range of food. A typical example is in the numbers of most owls that breed in the far north, and rough-legged buzzard, hen harrier and long-tailed skua, all of which specialize in catching small rodents (see p. 12). The fluctuations that occur, say, in the numbers of short-eared owls are not necessarily apparent in the tawny owl and eagle owl, which will also catch small rodents if there are any available, but can make do equally well with worms, insects and birds (tawny owl) and birds and hares (eagle owl).

The numbers of grouse and redpoll also depend on food supply. Grouse often lay a large number of eggs (as do all game birds) some time between late May and mid-June (grouse) or in June (ptarmigan). The hen birds and eggs can withstand severe cold and snow during hatching. The young are hatched in time for the 'mosquito season', some time after midsummer, when there is usually a perceptible rise in the numbers of mosquitoes and other insects (at different times at different altitudes, in keeping with the habitats chosen by the various species). The young chicks, however, are highly sensitive to damp and cold, both directly and indirectly – the latter because the weather affects the hatching of mosquitoes, their staple diet. Consequently, persistent rain and cold during early summer adversely affects the hatching of grouse species. The gyr falcon, a specialist in catching grouse, is also ultimately dependent on mosquitoes, as is the merlin, because the size of the mosquito population influences the numbers of passerines.

Fluctuations in the numbers of small rodents

Many predatory bird species depend on the supply of small rodents. Numbers of lemmings and voles fluctuate with a certain regularity. Most often there is a peak every three or four years, followed by a drastic decline. This regular pattern is often disrupted, however, and the various causative factors include: weather (snow conditions, melted snow flooding tunnels); interaction with vegetation (exhausted food resources); variations in the quality of plants (depending on climate or due to the animals, as their consumption of a large proportion of plant life releases nutrients via excrement and decayed bodies, and is thus available again to the plants); interaction with predatory animals or parasites and diseases; and self-regulating factors (stress, emigration). All these factors probably have an effect, jointly or separately, in different areas.

It is clear, however, that small mammal populations have a marked influence on birds of prey and some predatory mammals. There are several touches of genius in the way owls adjust to the variable supply of small rodents. For example, the number of eggs laid by the female will depend on the food available during winter and early spring. In very poor conditions she may not lay any eggs at all. The actual number can vary between none and fourteen, in the various owl species. The eggs are laid at intervals of one or a few days and incubated immediately, so that the hatching young are correspondingly spaced. This gives a ranking order in the nest – the oldest nestling is fed first and has the best chance of survival, then the next oldest and so on. If the supply of rodents deteriorates drastically, perhaps only one nestling will survive, and it often happens that one or more are eaten by the others. If the food supply is adequate, however, several or all of the young will fly. This arrangement improves the chances of at least one or two nestlings being successfully reared during bad rodent years. When the migrant short-eared owl returns in spring it will shun its traditional breeding grounds if there are no voles. The snowy, great grey and hawk owls emigrate when food is short.

The rodent peak can be confined to one species or it can involve

Grey-sided vole

Norway lemming

Common red-backed vole

several. When the Norway lemming, mostly found on bare mountains (although in peak years it migrates towards the trees), has a good year, there will also be plenty of long-tailed skuas and rough-legged buzzards, and usually some snowy owls and other species such as voles, living above the tree line. When the rodents in the forest zone are plentiful, the forest owl species thrive. The long-tailed skua can also migrate towards the forest zone if there is a better supply of voles. Similarly, the short-eared owl breeds in bogs and moorland above the tree line as well as in marshes and meadows well down in the forest zone. Practically all predatory animals (bears, foxes, wolverines) concentrate on catching small rodents during peak years, which eases the pressure on adult and young grouse, duck, wader and other species, which are thus also affected indirectly. The taking of voles during their peak years has other effects too. Some passerines, such as the redwing, then seem to build nests more commonly up in the vegetation as voles take eggs. The cropping of shrubs, berries and bark, which are heavy in some areas, should affect the insect population and the food supply available to birds; perhaps it means fewer berries and buds for grouse species during the following winter. Voles and lemmings, the principal northern rodents, feed mainly on leaves and stalks. Mice, such as long-tailed and yellow-necked fieldmice, eat more seeds and nuts and thus the fruit production of the spruce, pine, hazel and oak are important to them. Fieldmice do not penetrate to mountain regions or the northern part of the conifer zone, but the house mouse and brown rat occur close to houses and human settlement throughout northern Europe. Numbers of Norway lemmings probably vary most drastically. Some years they can almost engulf some mountain areas, and can cause considerable destruction in the sensitive alpine zone. Shrews, which are insectivores (their closest relative is the hedgehog), seem to make up a fairly minor part of the diet of predatory birds, even though they are common in the mountain and conifer zones.

A group of ptarmigan take advantage of a meagre midday sun to eat buds, shoots and berries exposed by the icy wind that sweeps across the bare mountain. The males have a black stripe running from the bill through the eye.

Birds in winter

How do birds survive in winter? Many species migrate to warmer areas where food is more plentiful. Geese, ducks and waders, which depend on water, are forced by the winter ice to migrate southwest to western Europe, the Mediterranean and western Africa. Most insectivorous birds must also migrate. Those that are able to stay on in the mountains and forest zones throughout the winter are the plant eaters and the birds which in their turn live on these birds and other animals. The ptarmigan stays on the bare mountain all through the winter because the wind clears the snow from vegetation on peaks and slopes. Among the plants that survive in such drastic weather conditions are crowberries, which are very important to all the grouse species. The extreme cold keeps berries and edible plants almost deep-frozen, so they retain their nourishment all through the winter. The short period of daylight at about noon during midwinter can at times be augmented by moonlight, which is greatly magnified by the white snow. Birch buds make up a large proportion of the winter diet of the willow grouse. The capercaillie feeds throughout the winter mainly on pine needles. Grouse, and probably the redpoll, dig themselves into the snow cover, an insulation from nocturnal temperatures of 30° to 40° C below zero. The golden eagle, raven and Siberian jay, like the fox and Arctic fox, feed on the remains of reindeer, elk and roe deer killed and partially eaten by larger predatory animals. The Siberian jay, like the tits, accumulates various stores of food during autumn and often hunts for scraps left by forestry workers. Tits, goldcrests and treecreepers often spend the night in holes, crevices and nesting boxes. Small rodents survive quite comfortably beneath the snow. The temperature in the soil stratum under a thick cover of snow remains quite constant at about 10° C. The Norway lemming even manages to produce several batches of young during favourable winters, which means that there is food for the owls. However, a rigorous selection process takes place during winter, and only the hardiest survive until the next breeding season.

Environmental problems

Large portions of the conifer zone in Fennoscandia are now being changed by man's interference. In recent years the forest environment has been radically transformed by modern techniques: increased felling completely clears large areas. Because these clear-felled areas are planted with young conifers and the hardwood trees eliminated with weedkillers, reafforestation results in monocultures – plantations of uniform age containing only one species (spruce or pine). This has a number of effects on birds – some thrive and others suffer.

Areas where trees have been felled receive much more sun and thus generate more abundant vegetation which, at least to begin with, increases the vole population. This in turn benefits owls, rough-legged buzzards and great grey shrikes, which will hunt in these areas. In the short term, the dead hardwood trees provide nesting places for some owl species and food (insect larvae) for woodpeckers. On the other hand, the long-term consequences are not yet fully known. If increasingly large areas of 'natural' forest (mixed forest with trees of different ages) are replaced by 'industrial' forests characterized by monoculture, artificial fertilization, chemical defoliation, widespread insecticide use and the absence of any old trees, this is likely to have adverse long-term consequences. Certain species (golden eagle, white-tailed eagle, goshawk, black woodpecker) need stout old trees for nests, while many owls need dead hollow trees. Monocultures, moreover, greatly increase the numbers of some harmful insects (weevils and bark beetles), with the result that pesticides (mainly DDT) become indispensable. Monocultures also have the disadvantage of being more

This is, unfortunately, an increasingly rare sight in northern Europe. A lone lesser white-fronted goose rests with two bean geese and two pairs of wigeon while they wait for the ice to melt high up in the mountains. For how many more years will the lesser white-fronted goose be classified as a species breeding in our area? Five? Ten?

sensitive to climatic change. Then again, it is becoming increasingly common in northern Europe to drain wet areas within forests to improve timber production. Waterlogged forests often have abundant flora and fauna and are a major breeding ground for many bird species in the conifer zone.

Forest timber must, of course, be economically exploited, but when it comes to natural resources we must also be guided by ecological sense. If 'reasonable' or 'necessary' interference with the forest environment refers to short-term profitability, this means sacrificing the equilibrium that has existed for thousands of years for cyclic fluctuations. The forest should be managed on its own terms. Greater expanses of unspoiled primitive forest should be preserved, and additional steps should be taken to safeguard the existing reserves.

Mountain ranges incorporate many irreplaceable areas of wilderness – a fast-dwindling environment in Europe and elsewhere in the world. Scientifically, ethically, and for recreational purposes, it is imperative that we preserve among the mountains a natural environment which is relatively unaffected by modern-day intrusions and still retains an abundant and original flora and fauna. It is alarming to note how little weight ecological arguments and the protected status of national parks carry when they are pitted against economic considerations. The construction of holiday homes, winter sports centres, road-building across virgin mountain areas and demands for increased hydro-electric power production are a threat to mountain regions and, ultimately, to ourselves.

Field identification and the outward structure of birds

Plumage

When looking at birds, one must know something of their outward structure, together with the ornithological terms of identification. Perhaps the most distinctive features of birds as an animal group are their ability to fly and that their bodies are covered with feathers. There are two main types of feathers: down and contour. The young of some species are covered with down when first hatched, so that they can retain their body heat. This is typical of species left alone in the nest at an early age (birds of prey and owls) and of those where the young emerge from the nest immediately (ducks, waders and game birds). Wing and tail feathers are one form (or type) of contour feathers, and the 'outer casing' of the fully grown bird consists of contours which conceal the underlying heat insulation of down. Many of the contours attached to the body also have a downy lower part, and some groups have an extra feather in the form of down attached to the base of the quill; this is the case with game birds. There is also half-down – something between down and feathers. Feathers are distributed in different areas called 'tracts' on the body which form more or less distinct parts of the outer shape and provide points of reference for plumage descriptions. They are illustrated on p. 19, together with other important parts and typical markings.

Moulting

Moulting is an important stage in a bird's annual cycle. Most species change their tail and wing feathers, certain body contours and the bastard wing once a year. Body feathers and, often, tertiaries and the central tail feathers are changed once or twice every year or, in exceptional cases, three times. Birds that change their body feathers twice-yearly include divers, dabbling ducks, many waders, gulls, terns, wagtails, pipits and warblers. The moulting process is often complex, and the basic 'timetable' of a species is also influenced by race, food supply and migration times. A knowledge of the moulting, such as season of year, the number of times per year and the order in which the different groups of feathers are shed often helps to identify different species. However, individuals in the process of moulting (in intermediate plumage), can often be seen at any time during the year.

Types of plumage

The first real set of feathers acquired after the initial down covering is called juvenile plumage. In some families, such as larks, pipits, thrushes and buntings, the feathers are somewhat different in structure – thinner, downier and less wear-resistant. Also, they are coloured to camouflage the young birds from predators. This plumage is usually soon replaced, partly or wholly, especially in passerines. The next plumage often results from a change of body feathers and some wing coverts, tertiaries and the central tail feathers (although game birds, larks and the bearded reedling change all their feathers). Ducks, for example, are at their most beautiful during winter, which is their mating season, and the first-winter plumage of surface-feeding ducks and some of the small diving ducks resembles the winter dress of the adults. However, young ducks acquire winter plumage later than their seniors, and sometimes it is not complete until midwinter. In many other species the adult's full colour stage is preceded by a varying number of immature dresses. This is a striking characteristic of predators and gulls. In species which change some or all of their body feathers twice a year, one can usually distinguish separate winter and summer plumages. This applies, for example, to divers, ducks, waders, gulls, terns and certain thrushes. Several passerines acquire summer dress by wearing away the edges of their feathers. The feathers of winter or autumn plumage, acquired between late summer and autumn, have very wide fringes which are gradually worn away to reveal the underlying, more brightly-coloured, plumage (bluethroat, brambling, Lapland bunting and snow bunting). In many species (whinchat, wheatear and Lapland bunting) this wear is accompanied by the moulting of certain groups of feathers. In short, three distinct plumages should be borne in mind:

Juvenile A bird is called juvenile (or immature) until it has begun to acquire its second set of wing feathers, but as used in this book the term indicates that a bird has its first proper plumage. Species shedding their body feathers once or twice before they change their wing feathers are juv. autumn, juv. first winter and so on.

Adult A bird is adult when it has acquired its full colouring. If the adult bird has two or more distinguishable plumages per year, these are termed ad. winter (autumn) and ad. summer (spring). Unless otherwise indicated, birds are illustrated in adult summer dress, or, with duck species, in winter dress.

Subadult A bird is subadult when it is neither juvenile nor fully coloured (adult). The term 'young bird' applies to all non-adults – both juveniles and subadults.

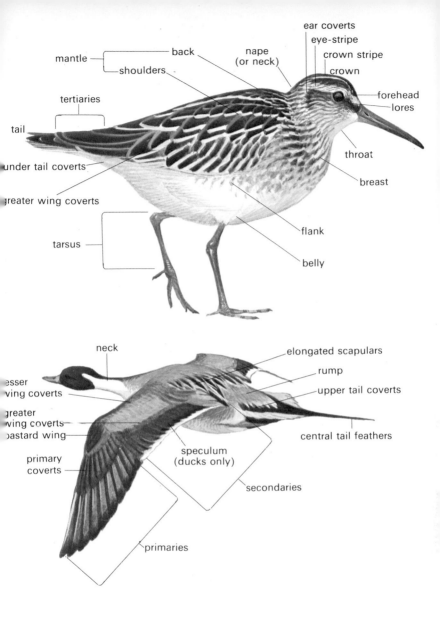

Top: broad-billed sandpiper in immature plumage. Bottom: pintail, seen overhead in winter plumage.

19

A lapland bunting (juvenile plumage) soon after leaving the nest.

Appearance and problems of field recognition

Appearance and plumages vary considerably within a species. Certain species, whatever their plumage, are conspicuously marked in one or several ways, which make them easily recognizable under most conditions. Others have markings that are not easy to identify and may show a good deal of individual variation, making field recognition difficult if not impossible. Individual young divers, ducks, harriers, falcons, larks, pipits, warblers and buntings are particularly difficult to identify in some plumages. The reader should consider nature's variety and changeability and treat the facts with patience, precision and a bit of imagination.

Calls and song

The ability to identify calls and song is an important aspect of field recognition and a big help in locating birds. In fact, the best way to recognize owls and waders is by their calls. The various calls each have a particular function or significance to members of the same species, and can be grouped according to their purpose. In many cases, however, the boundaries between these groups are flexible, which makes the following only a rough guide: song or mating call, summoning call, contact call, warning note, and begging and other calls. Among ducks, for instance, because visual signals are more important than vocal ones, the song, or rather the mating call, is usually the same as the contact or summoning call. In many cases the differences between the various summoning and contact calls are unclear. Some species – the yellow wagtail is one – have a whole repertoire of summoning calls. Contact calls are used to keep the flock together, and differ from summoning calls. In some species warning and summoning calls merge or are combined according to mood, while in other species they are quite different.

Behaviour, habitat and distribution

The behaviour and habitat of a bird are no less important a part of field recognition than its appearance and calls. A bird's choice of biotope is often a great help (see p. 10). For instance, is it found in a forest swamp or a mountain birch forest? On the other hand, any species can be expected to behave abnormally in unusual surroundings or circumstances. The distribution and, in the case of migrants, the occurrence of species in relation to the time of year, can be convincing evidence, or at least a clue, to its identity. You are unlikely to see a wood warbler in Britain in March, for example, because it seldom arrives before late April. On the other hand, occasional specimens of most species, especially migrants, are regularly observed far outside their normal distribution areas. The distribution areas of the various species are illustrated by maps, with a key (see below).

Population density varies considerably, and it should be noted that certain species can be extremely rare in large parts of their distribution areas. Moreover, populations can also vary a great deal from year to year (see p. 11). Breeding areas, however, are usually more constant than wintering areas.

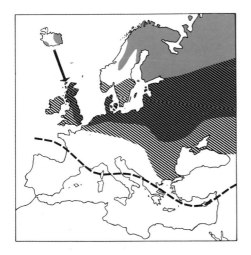

Blue: nests, summer visitor only
Blue dot: breeds occasionally; isolated colonies
Blue and shading: nests and winters
Shading: winter visitor
Arrow: principal migration routes
Broken line: irregular winter visitor

21

Red-throated diver
juv. winter

Black-throated diver
juv. winter

Black-throated diver
ad. winter

Red-throated diver *Gavia stellata* 53–69 cm

Prefers nesting beside small pools in tundra and open moorland. One can venture very near the nest, but the bird tries to avoid discovery by submerging, laying its head on the water's surface so that only the bill and crown are visible. The russet throat patch may be seen at close quarters, but from a distance on open water the silhouette is more conspicuous, with an angular head shape, more upright posture and 'sharper' beak. Fishes in large lakes within its breeding area or at sea, and is frequently seen – or, rather, heard – in flight. When flying, often at a great height, it emits a noisy goose-like clamour, 'kak-kak-kak', in time with the wing beats. On the water there is also a protracted wailing 'eeaaoh'. Its mating call is a long-drawn-out 'kor-korroi, kor-korroi ...' The young have a much paler throat and head than the black-throated and small pale patches on their upper parts.

Black-throated diver *Gavia arctica* 58–73 cm

Less Arctic in habitat than the red-throated diver. Nests mainly in clear deep lakes and is sometimes seen in northern areas with red-throated divers. However, the black-throated has a more serpentine neck and head, with the head held more upright and the top of the bill more arched. In winter plumage the upper parts are darker than the red-throated, with a distinct border to the white underparts of throat and head. The young are somewhat lighter, with a pale grey bill. The mating call is a sequence of melodious and melancholy phrases which can be heard from a long distance – 'kok-klauik, kok-klaui-kok-klaui ...' It also has a raucous 'oo-aaoh' and deep growling notes. Usually silent in flight, but sometimes emits a cackle like the red-throated. Often difficult to distinguish from the red-throated in flight, but the throat is slightly thicker and there are wider dark bars along the sides of the body at the wing base. The diet is the same as the red-throated.

Red-throated diver

Black-throated diver

Red-throated diver

Black-throated diver

Geese, swans and ducks   *Anatidae*

Geese, swans and ducks form a characteristic feature of the northern wetlands. Twenty-eight of the forty species regularly found in Europe breed entirely or partly within the Arctic region and/or the northern conifer belt. The many lakes and watercourses and extensive swamps and deltas with abundant insects and fish-spawn (mosquito larvae are particularly important in the diet) provide excellent breeding conditions. These birds are especially adapted to life on the water: flat, boat-shaped bodies, dense, highly water-repellent plumage over a thick layer of down, webbed feet and long necks. Both duck sexes have a most handsome courtship plumage in winter (more distinctive in the male), another from early summer and, during high summer and autumn, a less conspicuously marked eclipse or summer dress which in both sexes usually resembles the female in winter. Tail and wing feathers, replaced during the eclipse period, are shed so quickly that for a short period the birds cannot fly. The down-covered young are able to swim soon after hatching and can find their own food with the mother's guidance. *Anatidae* are grouped as follows:

Swans (*Cygninae*). Of the three species, the mute swan has been introduced into parts of Europe, while the two vocal swan species breed in Arctic or northern areas.

Geese (*Anserinae*). Except for the greylag goose (and the Canada goose, an introduced species) all eight species occurring in Europe breed in Arctic latitudes, although the majority breed in Greenland, Spitsbergen or the tundras of northern Asia.

Dabbling ducks (*Anatinae*) occur mainly in fresh water especially in eutrophic and shallow areas. They graze on aquatic plants by 'up-ending' in shallow water, or dabble or filter small creatures and parts of plants from the water's surface. Take-off from the water is almost vertical. In addition to the species mentioned here, the mallard (*Anas platyrhynchos*) is common in lakes high in the birch zone, the gadwall (*A. strepera*) occurs locally in the Lake Myvatn area of Iceland and the shoveler (*A. clypeata*) inhabits shallow eutrophic lakes as far north as the 66th parallel.

Diving ducks (*Aythyinae*) dive for most of their food, pattering along the water surface with their short wings beating before taking off.

Smaller diving ducks usually breed beside fresh water and are also found in central and southern Europe. There are seven species, of which the tufted duck, scaup, goldeneye and Barrow's goldeneye breed within the area.

Sea ducks breed along sea coasts and beside clear mountain and tundra lakes, and winter mainly by the sea. Of the seven European species, the velvet scoter, common scoter, harlequin and long-tailed duck breed beside inland lakes, watercourses and the sea, while the other three – eider, king eider and Steller's eider – inhabit sea coasts, especially of the Arctic Ocean, where they breed in small expanses of water. Sawbills (*Merginae*), with long, slender, toothed bills, are adept fish hunters. They rise from the water like diving ducks. All three European species breed in the same area as the other divers.

Opposite: chicks of duck species

Teal

Pintail

Wigeon

Tufted duck

Scaup

Goosander

Red-breasted merganser

Goldeneye

Smew

Barrow's goldeneye

Harlequin

Velvet scoter

Long-tailed duck

Common scoter

Whooper swan   *Cygnus cygnus*

145–160 cm

Nests in marshy lakes in tundra and forest country. In recent years it has spread south, while the mute swan has advanced to the north. The Asian tundra from the Kola Peninsula eastwards is the breeding ground of Bewick's swan (*C. bewickii*), which is slightly smaller and has less yellow on its bill. The whooper swan migrates south in family groups when the lakes freeze over. In spring, even before the ice breaks up, pairs are stationed beside their breeding lakes. Throughout the winter and spring it is highly vociferous, with a melodious and resonant 'clong' and short trumpet blasts. A pair of whooper swans will display to each other with erect bodies, necks outstretched and wings flapping. Close to the nest they are sometimes notably aggressive towards geese and divers. The whooper swan feeds on aquatic plants, but also grazes on the shore.

Lesser white-fronted goose   *Anser erythropus*   53–66 cm

Numbers have declined disastrously in the Scandinavian mountain range during the past few decades. It is now a very rare breeder beside lakes in the osier and birch region. A shy bird, it is difficult to locate in the osier jungles, its favourite habitat. Despite its smallness, it is hard to distinguish in flight from other geese, for example the bean goose, except by its voice. The young have the typical pale eye-ring (see p. 16) but do not have a white forehead. The flight call is much louder than other geese, 'djee-yee' or 'djee-yeek', while the warning call is a very loud, somewhat grating 'queue-oop'. Migrates to the southeast and returns in May, but may pause in hay fields and marshes in coastal areas and river valleys until the snow melts on the mountains. Various plants make up its diet.

Whooper swan

Lesser white-fronted goose

Pink-footed goose

Bean goose

Pink-footed goose *Anser brachyrhynchus* 60–75 cm

Possibly a race of bean goose, it breeds only in eastern Greenland, Spitsbergen and interior Iceland. The birds from Spitsbergen migrate through Norway to Denmark and the North Sea coasts, while the western populations mainly winter in eastern Scotland and, in smaller numbers, further south. Smaller than the bean goose, it has shorter pink legs, a shorter neck, a rounder head and a shorter (also pink) bill. It makes a paler, more grey and fawn/pink impression, the flanks and neck being the darkest parts of the body. The wings, mantle and rear part of the back look very pale in flight, and the tail has a thicker white border compared with the bean goose. The drab dark young often have fawnish legs. Like the bean goose, old birds may have a white border or a narrow white patch at the bill base. The note is higher and shriller than the bean goose's but diet and winter habitat are similar.

Bean goose *Anser fabalis* 66–84 cm

An occasional breeder in swamps and river deltas in the northern parts of the coniferous region. Very shy in its breeding grounds, and difficult to spot. In spring it rests at the same time as whooper swans beside openings in the ice, or on snow-free reaches of the great northern rivers – for example, on banks near hydro-electric power stations that have been cleared of ice and snow. It spends the night on islets or osier banks that are surrounded by water, and morning or evening can be seen or heard flying to its grazing grounds. Its note is an elastic nasal cackling 'kayak' or 'kayakak'. Large flocks migrate in autumn from the Asian taiga to Europe, pausing in fields and pastures en route. Feeds on various plants.

Pink-footed goose

Bean goose

juvenile

Pink-footed goose

Bean goose

juvenile

Pintail ♀　　　Wigeon

Wigeon   *Anas penelope*   45–51 cm

Found beside lakes, wetlands and river deltas with grassy shores. The breeding areas range from the birch belt to the coast. Lives mainly on grass and is often seen, like geese, grazing in pairs. Outside the mating season the birds are highly gregarious, and a flock is easily recognized, even at a distance. They keep close together but in outline have relatively long tails, round heads and long wings. The adult drake's white wing patches can be seen from a great distance, and the clearly delineated white belly is a characteristic of all age groups. Year-old drakes have only a vague, dingy white wing patch. A pleasant whistle of wings accompanies the flock in flight. The silhouette, relatively similar to the diving duck's, is also a distinguishing feature on the water, and the ducklings, too, look very much like diving ducks. The drake's mating call is a tuneful whistling 'hui-oo', often heard in winter. The duck has a hoarse 'oarr, oarr, oarr . . .' like the diving duck females. Towards late summer the flocks, in close formation, pause in fertile lakes on their journey south and crop the aquatic plants. They are in eclipse at this time, in shades varying from the dull brownish-grey of the ducks to the wine red of the older drakes.

Pintail   *Anas acuta*   ♂61–76 cm ♀51–57 cm

The long neck and tail make the pintail easy to spot. The slim body lines and the speculum's pale rear edge are distinguishing features in flight. Compared with the mallard, ducks and immatures have a greyer base colour and are more finely spotted, with the markings more evenly distributed. The main breeding haunts are flat marshes and deltas in the tundra, taiga and moorland and often beside swampy lakes. The drake's mating call is a teal-like 'krily'. The female has a croaking note like the mallard's but lower in pitch, and a wigeon-like grating note. The diet is green plants and seeds.

Wigeon

Pintail

♀

Wigeon

♂

♀

Pintail

♂

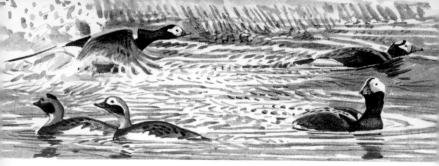

Long-tailed duck

Teal *Anus crecca* 34–38 cm

The only dabbling duck of its size in the region. Usually nests beside lakes and river deltas from the coastal marshes far into the willow region. Prefers shallow waters, especially those surrounded by woodland or bushes, and often breeds beside small forest tarns or rivers. Springs readily off the water and is noisy in flight. The drake has a melodious, short, clearly-ringing 'krrip'. The duck has a bright shrill croak and, when taking to the wing, a subdued grating 'trrr'. Lives on plants, seeds and some aquatic insects.

Long-tailed duck *Clangula hyemalis* ♂58–60 cm ♀37–41 cm

Breeds beside small lakes and rivers in the tundra and mountains, mainly in the birch and willow region, and along the Arctic coast, often in small lakes near the coast. Rare in the southern part of its distribution area, its numbers have probably declined in recent decades due, among other things, to increasing oil pollution in its wintering places. Towards late summer the drake goes into eclipse, with brownish-grey shoulder feathers and dingy grey sides. Winter plumage is like a photographic negative of the spring dress, with dark turned into light and vice versa. During the breeding season many birds retain a white patch at the back of the head. The ducks vary quite considerably but are much paler during the winter. Immatures have more regular markings and a dingier, more uniformly dull appearance. Throughout spring and early summer the drake emits a loud, beautiful, almost feline 'au-au-li' or 'a-a-auli'. Because it often breeds on very small areas of water, there are frequent and protracted hostilities between drakes. Winters are spent in the open sea, often as far north as the ice permits. Animal food is the main diet, with ant larvae an important addition in the breeding grounds.

Teal

Long-tailed duck

Teal ♀

♂

♂

♀

Long-tailed duck

Scaup in winter dress: one ad. ♂, two year-old ♂ ♂ and one ♀. The sleeping bird is a tufted duck ♀

Tufted duck   *Aythya fuligula*   40–47 cm

Often seen on natural and artificial waters in towns and close to human settlement, its original distribution was northern, but recently there has been a considerable southerly expansion in its range. It breeds beside relatively shallow lakes with abundant vegetation, or in small tarns and river deltas up to the willow region. Sometimes breeds alongside the scaup, although the latter ventures further up to the most inhospitable mountain lakes. The tuft, less pronounced in the duck, distinguishes this bird from the scaup, as does the black mantle of the drake. The white patch at the bill base is variable in females of both species, but is rarely so extensive in tufted as in scaup. The drake's courtship call is a long vibrant whistling, while the duck's note is a fierce growling 'err, err, err . . .'

Scaup   *Aythya marila*   42–51 cm

A rare breeding bird except in the north of our region, it nests beside clear lakes bordered by sedge in mountainous birch and willow regions. Scaup are usually encountered in pairs or small groups, when they are easily recognizable from tufted ducks by the mottled grey upper parts of the drake and larger rounder heads. The duck has a speckled grey mantle during the winter, but towards early summer she turns a more uniform brown and develops a variable white patch on her ear coverts as well as the white face patch. The drake in eclipse is 'mangier' with dingy mottled flanks and duck-like pale markings around the bill base. His courtship note is a short deep whistling 'peho'. The duck's hoarse note is similar to the tufted duck's 'err . . . err . . .' The summer diet is freshwater insects, molluscs, crustaceans and some seeds.

Tufted duck

Scaup

Tufted duck

♂

♂

Scaup

♂

♀

Scaup

♀

♀

Tufted duck ♀

Velvet scoter ♀   Common scoter ♂

Common scoter   *Melanitta nigra*   44–54 cm

Relatively common from the upper coniferous belt to the willows in the north of the region. Breeds in higher-altitude lakes than the velvet scoter. The male is easily distinguished from the velvet scoter because it has no white markings. The dark brown female has a dark patch over her head (otherwise strikingly pale) and the sides of the neck. The paler grey feather edges give the body a dappled look. The male has a very distinctive, short whistling 'pyu' or 'pyoo-pyoo', the female a dark noisy 'hau (haurr) ... hau ... hau'. On take-off the wings sound like tinkling ice because of the unusually shaped primaries. During spring common scoters may be seen migrating in dense flocks, straggling low over the sea in the south, but mostly at night and over land as they near their breeding grounds. The diet is mainly molluscs, crustaceans and insects.

Velvet scoter   *Melanitta fusca*   51–58 cm

Breeds by clear mountain lakes and also, commonly, along the Baltic coasts. Compared with the common scoter it seldom ventures as far as the tree line but is commonest on the margins between the coniferous and birch regions. It tends to nest under a tree or bush, often some distance from water. In preparation for nesting, which starts about midsummer, the pair stake their claim by flying around their territory; at this time the female emits a nasal rolling 'arr-ha' and her wings make a soft whistling sound. Both sexes and all ages have a large white speculum which remains partially visible when they sit on the water. Some females lack the pale head marking, but the flat forehead and less vertical bill base distinguish them from the common scoter. The diet is the same as the common scoter's.

Common scoter

Velvet scoter

Common scoter

Velvet scoter

Goldeneye

Smew

Goldeneye   *Bucephala clangula*   42–50 cm

A widespread breeding bird beside lakes and running water in the coniferous belt. Nests in hollow trees, nesting boxes, even in the abandoned nesting holes of black woodpeckers. Females and young may be seen on very small tarns, but they prefer larger open waters, especially rivers and rapids. The goldeneye's closest relative, Barrow's goldeneye, does not breed in Europe outside Iceland, which makes identification simpler. The young, generally darker than older birds, do not have yellow on the bill or white on the throat. When the ice breaks up and goldeneyes return to their nesting places the males enthusiastically perform their courtship ceremonies. They throw back their heads, stretch them on the water's surface and reach upwards with their bills while emitting a fast 've-veyeck' followed by a creaking twitter. The female's note is a fast-rolling 'berr, berr, berr'. The male also makes a pleasant whistling sound with his wings. The goldeneye dives for molluscs, crustaceans and insect larvae in relatively deep water.

Smew   *Mergus albellus*   38–44 cm

Biotope requirements and nesting biology are very much like the goldeneye's. They are sometimes observed side by side and even produce hybrids, but the smew is a rarer breeder in our area. The female could be mistaken for a goldeneye except for her distinctive white cheeks. The parallel development of the two species is even more apparent from their newly-hatched young (p. 25). The male in eclipse resembles the female. His splendid plumage is not acquired until late autumn. In flight the smew is easily distinguished from diving and surface-feeding ducks by its slender shape and fast easy movement. The wing patch on the lesser coverts – large and bright white in the male and greyish white in the female – resembles the wigeon's and is another distinguishing feature in flight. The smew lives mainly on fish and other aquatic creatures.

Goldeneye

Smew

Goldeneye

♀

♂

♂

♀

Smew

Red-breasted merganser ♀   Goosander ♀

Red-breasted merganser   *Mergus serrator*   51–62 cm

Breeds fairly commonly beside clear lakes and rivers up to the willow zone, but more commonly near sea coasts. Prefers rocky streams and likes to nest on open grass-grown islets. During winter, this bird is seldom seen on fresh water. In summer the male has an eclipse plumage resembling the female's, but retains his white lesser wing coverts, a darker and browner mantle and redder eyes. Young males in late winter acquire a touch of black in their plumage and crests and occasional black or white body feathers. The female differs from the female goosander by the even transition between brown cap and white throat, a slimmer and more ragged crest and a less tapered bill. When the female takes to the wing there may be a dull rasping 'shrrk, shrrk, shrrk ...' These birds nest in midsummer or later. They patrol just offshore, plunging their heads in and out in search of fish.

Goosander   *Mergus merganser*   58–72 cm

Nests in hollow trees, and sometimes nesting boxes, near clear lakes and rivers in forested country in much the same habitat as goldeneye. Most birds winter on fresh waters, especially reservoirs, but sometimes along coasts. Arrives early in spring on the breeding grounds, often while the ice is breaking up. By this time partners have been chosen, and courtship display is losing intensity. During display the male quickly stretches his head straight up, emitting a distinctive and beautiful ringing note like the distant call of a crane. The couple then fly in large circles in search of a nest site, accompanied by a raucous rolling 'skrrak, skrrak, skrraak ...' from the female. In winter and spring both sexes have a pinkish flush over the white parts of their bodies, but this soon fades. The male in eclipse resembles the female. Immatures are like the female but have a pale line from the eye to the bill base. The goosander, with his narrow serrated beak, is mainly a fish-eater. Birds which are not nesting sometimes use a special hunting technique – they advance in a long line to beat a shoal of fish into a cove or inlet so that they can dive and catch them easily.

Red-breasted merganser

Goosander

Red-breasted merganser

Goosander

Goldeneye
young ♂ moulting

♂

♀

Barrow's goldeneye
young ♂ moulting

young ♀ moulting

♀ summer

♂

Barrow's goldeneye *Bucephala islandica* 42–53 cm

The main habitat is in North America, but this bird is also found in Iceland where it breeds commonly beside small lakes and rivers in the lava areas. It is numerous around Lake Myvatn where the fields of solidified lava provide nesting cavities, and the unusually warm water from the hot springs produces enormous amounts of mosquito and gnat larvae, the staple food of the newly-hatched young. Barrow's goldeneye is larger than the goldeneye, and males, females and the young can all be identified by their steep foreheads and short but deep bills.

Harlequin *Histrionicus histrionicus* 38–45 cm

Like Barrow's goldeneye, harlequin is a North American Arctic bird with its most
eastern outpost in Iceland. It breeds fairly commonly throughout Iceland where
it prefers fast-flowing water. Outside the breeding season it occurs along craggy
coasts. Only the males frequent the breeding grounds during spring and early
summer. When disturbed they fly into waterfalls or drift downstream, often swiftly,
so could be hard to spot. The flight is easy, rapid and darting. Females often have
completely dark wings, and immatures look almost like adults. Harlequins live on
insect larvae, molluscs, crustaceans and other small creatures that fasten onto stream
beds or rocks in the sea.

Golden eagle

Rough-legged buzzard

Gyr falcon

Hen harrier

Goshawk

Birds of prey   Order *Falconiformes*

Predators devour live birds, other animals and some carrion. Their flying skill, hooked bills, strong legs and feet, and sharp talons are ideal adaptations to this diet. The differences between the species reflect their food preferences and behaviour patterns. The relatively small bills and mode of flight of rough-legged buzzards and hen harriers suit their diet of small rodents. (See Introduction for small mammal population influence on predators.) Gyr falcon and merlin are fast strong fliers with relatively large feet to hunt down grouse and passerines. The huge golden eagle, with its stout bill, feet and legs, can capture and hold hares and foxes.

Predators are often seen in flight from a great distance, which sometimes makes their colour and size difficult to judge. Therefore, silhouette, flight, movements and general behaviour are important identifying characteristics. Notice, for example, how the gyr falcon, when gliding or riding on upward airstreams, tends to curve its wings upwards and let its tail hang down, while the goshawk glides with wings held rigid and curved slightly downwards, and the hen harrier and golden eagle most often plane and glide with their wings forming a V.

Birds of prey are divided into two sub-orders. *Accipitres* includes the osprey and hawk-like birds and the *Falcones* are falcons. Hawk-like predators are divided into kites, vultures, short-toed eagles, harriers, hawks, buzzards and eagles. Apart from the species included here, white-tailed eagle (see under golden eagle), peregrine falcon (see gyr falcon) and kestrel (see merlin) also breed in mountain areas above the conifer line and in the tundra. Osprey, black kite, honey buzzard, goshawk (see gyr falcon), sparrow hawk (see merlin) and buzzard (see rough-legged buzzard) also breed in the relatively far north of the conifer belt.

Hen harrier

Hen harrier *Circus cyaneus*

43–50 cm
wing span 100–120 cm

The only harrier that breeds in the northern coniferous belt. In the British Isles it nests in young conifer plantations and open moorland in the north. In the taiga it is relatively common in open country with swamps and hay fields, and is often found on ditched walls. In our area, however, the actual nest is built in thin marshy woodland. With wings held high it gracefully glides near the ground. The female could be taken for a short-eared owl or a rough-legged buzzard, but the gull-like bluish grey of the male is highly distinctive. In spring the male performs an aerial courtship ritual, steeply climbing and falling and sometimes tumbling or gyrating around his own axis while emitting a dry chattering 'chuck-uck-uck-uck-uck'. The female's supplicating note when the male arrives with food is a bright hoarse 'pih-e' and her warning call is an agitated 'check-eck-eck-eck …' similar to the great spotted woodpecker. As the main diet is mice and voles, the number of nesting birds often depends on the supply of rodents.

Rough-legged buzzard, hovering

Rough-legged buzzard *Buteo lagopus*

53–64 cm
wing span 130–150 cm

Feeds almost entirely on small rodents, and in years when the supply is good it is commonly seen in undulating mountain areas above the conifer line, and less often in forest country. The wide population fluctuations of rough-legged buzzards and rodents do not always coincide completely, however, because of climate and other factors. This bird often hovers or, given a favourable wind, rides with wings held rigid, on a southern slope just above the mountain ridge. Its colour, markings and size vary a good deal and some individuals, particularly older ones, can easily be mistaken for buzzards.

The buzzard (*B. buteo*) 51–56 cm, wing span 114–133 cm is widespread in Europe and Asia but does not venture as far north as the tundra. Its northern boundary is the coniferous region, where its breeding grounds are close to open fields and swamps.

The buzzards nesting in northern Scandinavia and further east belong to the race *vulpinus*. They are slightly smaller than those to the south and west in Europe and more often than not have a touch of brownish red and a tail shaded between a lighter beige and rust red, with faint dark bars.

The rough-legged buzzard differs from the buzzard in that it has longer wings and often hovers. When the perching rough-legged buzzard is seen from close quarters, its feather-clad legs make positive identification possible. The facial expression formed partly by the slender bill, pale forehead and dark patch under the bill is also a striking characteristic. Young rough-legged buzzards are best distinguished in autumn by clearly defined pitch-black belly patches and a wide blackish-brown bar on the tail's outer edge, but these features can vary considerably. The note is a buzzard-like 'pieeeh', although weaker and more plaintive. Rough-legged buzzards migrate south or southeast in September and October, and may sometimes be numerous in areas where they are normally rarely seen. Voles, lemmings and mice make up almost their entire diet during the nesting season, although in certain years it includes young hares and young pheasants.

Rough-legged buzzard

Buzzard

Buzzard

adult

Rough-legged buzzard

juvenile

adult

adult

Rough-legged buzzard

adult

Golden eagle
juvenile

Golden eagle *Aquila chrysaetos*

76–89 cm
wing span 190–227 cm

The golden eagle often takes the observer by surprise – a dark shadow quickly looms up over the mountain ridge, or a dot moves slowly beneath the edge of a cloud a mile or so away. This bird is distinguished by a magnificent and beautifully-proportioned predator silhouette: its long tail and long, graceful, flexible wings are held in a shallow V when gliding or circling. Older birds have completely dark underparts and dappled light ochre, grey and dark brown upper parts. Younger birds are dark chocolate brown with white wing patches and a white tail base which can be seen from a considerable distance.

Nests are on remote rocky ledges and in large pine trees. Older pairs usually winter in the breeding area, in which case carrion are an important part of their diet. Otherwise they feed on hares, small rodents and birds, onto which they can swoop from a great height or take by surprise when flying at a low altitude. From late autumn onwards the pair perform flight displays in which the male pretends to attack the female: they tumble around together as they drop towards the ground, sometimes emitting a resonant `klyi`. The golden eagle population has declined considerably during the past century, partly due to pollution, modern forestry techniques, egg collecting and shooting or poisoning by over-zealous shepherds and gamekeepers.

The white-tailed eagle (*Haliaeetus albicilla*) also breeds along the Arctic coasts of Norway and Russia, in western Iceland and, rarely, in the interior of Lapland. It has a slightly larger wing span than the golden eagle and can be recognized by the horizontal posture of its wide rectangular wings when circling and gliding. It has a shorter, distinctly wedge-shaped tail – white in adults and dark in younger birds – and a thicker, more projecting head and bill.

Golden eagle

adult moulting

adult

juvenile

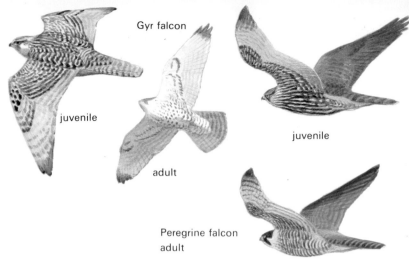

Gyr falcon

juvenile

adult

juvenile

Peregrine falcon
adult

Gyr falcon *Falco rusticolus*

55–60 cm
wing span 125–132 cm

The gyr falcon, mainly an Arctic predator, breeds in the tundra and high mountains around the entire northern hemisphere. It is as large and heavy as a female goshawk and could be confused with it or the peregrine falcon (*F. peregrinus*). It differs from the latter in that it is larger and longer, has a wider tail and wings and slower wing beats. It also lacks the clear black moustache of the peregrine falcon which, because of chemical pollution, is now represented in much of Europe by greatly reduced populations of nesting pairs. The markings of the gyr falcon vary, and some with colouring similar to the snowy owl can be seen in Greenland, while the gyr falcons of Iceland are, on average, paler than those in Scandinavia. It lives almost entirely on grouse and thus can stay in Arctic areas throughout the year. In Iceland other birds such as the golden plover and whimbrel probably make up an important part of its diet. Young birds (blue feet and cere) in particular move south towards the coast in late autumn. The warning call is a rough penetrating 'kerra-kerra-kerra ...'

The distribution of the goshawk (*Accipiter gentilis*) in northern Europe follows the northern boundary between the coniferous region and the tundra and high mountains. Although a typical forest bird, it has no objection to hunting over open mountainsides or coastal marshes. The wing motions are like the gyr falcon's, but are made by shorter wings with wider, more rounded tips. The goshawks breeding in the most northern areas of Europe, especially Siberia, are bigger and paler than southern populations and thus are more easily mistaken for the gyr falcon.

adult

adult

Gyr falcon

adult

juvenile

Kestrel

Sparrow hawk

Merlin

Merlin *Falco columbarius* 25–30 cm, wing span 60–65 cm

The merlin, and the small birds it specializes in catching, arrive and migrate at the same time. Nesting periods also coincide, so that young merlins feed on the young passerines which have just learned to fly and are still easy to catch. The merlin is small and thus easily recognized (the largest are the size of a stock dove) by its compact silhouette which does not have the elegance usually associated with falcons. The male is smaller than the female, with tinges of greyish blue and rust. The female usually has dark brown upper parts (although sometimes they may be rather greyish) and very mottled underparts. The markings of the sparrow hawk (p. 44) are similar except for the bars across its underparts. It also has a longer wider tail and shorter wider wings with distinct 'fingers' (splayed primary points). The merlin breeds in areas of mountain birch forest where it is locally common, and on treeless moorland. It often builds in old crows' nests or directly on the ground.

The merlin dive-bombs intruders who come close to its nest, circling with short, fast, vibrant wing beats while constantly emitting a rapid 'kikikiki ...' In autumn and winter it can be seen in open fields and marshes efficiently hunting pipits, buntings and finches, usually taking them by surprise on a fast arrow-like flight close to the ground.

The kestrel (*F. tinnunculus*) also breeds commonly in the same areas, but lives on rodents and insects. It has a 'thin' profile with a conspicuously long tail and reddish-brown (male) to fawn-brown (female) upper parts. Its flight is less dynamic, and it frequently hovers or perches on top of a tree, fence post or pylon on the lookout for prey.

Merlin

♂

♂

juvenile

♀

♀

courtship flight
cock bird, spring

Willow grouse cock, summer

Ptarmigan cock, summer

Ptarmigan   *Lagopus mutus*   35 cm

In certain plumages the willow grouse and ptarmigan look alike, but in winter they mostly form separate flocks, making the male ptarmigan's black rein (lacking in the females) a useful guidance feature. However, males of both species have at least four dress changes and the females have three, an effective blend into the surrounding colour and snow patterns. In summer and autumn the male ptarmigan is greyer than the willow grouse. Female summer dress varies but is paler yellowish grey with more irregular speckled markings than the willow grouse, with large dark mantle patches and an uneven transition to the paler belly. In autumn the sexes are similarly coloured. The male's note when taking to the wing is a dry rattling 'hurr-hurrrr', like the male garganey, and his courtship calls are similar. The female's note is a low 'kuck'. In the nesting season they usually occur far above the tree line in scree and boulder country, and are often relatively unafraid and even obtrusive when the young are nearby. Feeds on insects, berries and buds, but the chicks depend on insects, so persistent rain and cold in early summer much reduce the species.

Willow grouse/red grouse   *Lagopus lagopus*   40 cm

The willow grouse of continental Europe is bigger and slightly more elongated than the ptarmigan. In spring and autumn the male has liver-red to greyish-brown red dress. During the spring courtship period the otherwise completely white male has a liver-red head, throat and breast. In summer the female differs from the ptarmigan, with heavier and more uniform markings and a deeper shade of fawn – partly brick-coloured – but there is much individual variation. In the British Isles this species is represented by the red grouse (*L. lagopus scoticus*) which lacks a white winter plumage and has reddish-brown wings throughout the year. The red grouse breeds on large moorlands. The male's somewhat hysterical laughing note has an uncannily human ring, and quite often gives the mountain rambler a nasty fright. It is a nasally nagging, somewhat frog-like 'veugh vehehuhuhuhu', and the mating call is a succession of similar but steadily accelerating croaks.

   (*Distribution maps on p. 57*)

♂ summer

Ptarmigan

♂ spring

♂ winter
Ptarmigan

Willow grouse
winter

♂ spring

Willow grouse

♂ autumn

♀ summer

Ptarmigan

juvenile

♂ autumn

♀ summer

Willow grouse

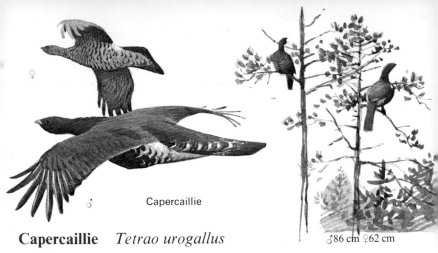

Capercaillie

Capercaillie *Tetrao urogallus*

♂86 cm ♀62 cm

This large grouse-like bird breeds in conifer woods and forests in northern Scotland and throughout the northern conifer belt. Often encountered at high altitudes towards the mountain birch belt, and in berry-rich swamps and forest bogs. When taking to the wing the female has a rounded, dark brownish-red tail which distinguishes her from the female black grouse (greyhen) whose tail is slightly cleft and brownish.

The black grouse (*Lyrurus tetrix*) breeds fairly commonly in the conifer belt. The cock bird (blackcock), about half the size of a male capercaillie, has a lyre-shaped tail and a white wing bar along the greater coverts.

Crane *Grus grus* (*illustrated on p. 58*)

114–130 cm
wing span 200–230 cm

Easy to identify, but during the nesting season it leads a withdrawn and very secretive life in remote peat bogs and marshes. The note may betray a couple, particularly at dawn when they perform their 'krrui-krroh, krrui-krroh' in a duet. Similar loud, nasal and grating bugle calls are emitted in flight. During spring the pair or the northward-moving flock perform the well-known ceremonial dance: bowing, raising the 'ostrich plumes' of their rear parts and bouncing into the air with wings held high. The suggestion of yellow brown on the mantle is thought to be muck deliberately smeared on with the bill, to better blend into the surroundings. Families migrate towards late summer, often pausing in the same stubble fields and pastures every year. Year-olds can then be identified by their uniformly brownish-grey plumage and the rather ostrich-like sculptured head shapes. Feeds on insects, small animals, fledglings and seeds.

Ptarmigan

Willow grouse

Crane

Crane

Waders and gulls Order *Charadriiformes*

Together with the auks, these two groups make up the order *Charadriiformes*. Like geese, swans and ducks, the **wader** group is associated with water and is numerous in Arctic areas. Of the forty or so species regularly occurring in Europe, twenty-nine breed partially or exclusively in Arctic areas. This applies to all small wader species (*Calidris* and *Limicola* families). Many of these, however, breed in the Arctic tundra of Asia and in Greenland and Spitsbergen. Waders are commonly divided into the following families: thick-knees, pratincoles, oystercatchers, plovers, phalaropes, stilts and avocets, and a miscellaneous family (*Scolopacidae*) of snipe, curlews, godwits and sandpipers of the two families *Calidris* and *Limicola*.

Gulls are divided into skuas (*Stercorariidae* family) and gulls and terns (*Laridae*). Skuas, gulls and terns, also widespread in northern areas, are mainly associated with sea coasts. The long-tailed skua differs from the others – it breeds on mountain heaths whether or not there is water nearby. The Pomarine skua (*Stercorarius pomarinus*) breeds in the tundra from the White Sea eastwards. Like the long-tailed skua, it depends on the lemming supply during the breeding season. It is one and a half times as large as the long-tailed skua and has 5 cm to 7.5 cm long tail projections with twisted and lumpy-looking tips.

Ringed plover   *Charadrius hiaticula*   19 cm

Sometimes it seems rather odd to see a ringed plover in mountain country, miles
away from any sea coast. But the fact is that it breeds regularly on gravel ridges in
the lichen zone and, locally, on river sandbanks at lower altitudes. The birds breeding
in the north belong to the race *tundrae* and have dark brownish-grey upper parts.
The boundary with the southern race is variable. In the mountains – unlike the
Baltic coasts and western Europe – it is the sole representative of the plover family.
The note is a soft whistling 'tu-ip' and the courtship flight is performed with slow
stiff wing beats to a crooning yodelling 'tack-aly, tack-aly, tack-aly ...' On the
ground it also emits a rolling 'kurrio-kurrio-kurrio ...' Unlike the southern race,
the northern ringed plover sometimes perches on a rock or similar strategic vantage
point. It lives on arthropods, worms and molluscs. (See distribution map p. 60.)

Golden plover

Dotterel

Dotterel   *Eudromias morinellus*   24 cm

This bird's colouring blends well with the shades and patterns on the mountain-top
but the eye-stripes and band on the breast are conspicuous from a distance. In
flight, the absence of wing bars and the dark patch on the belly are characteristic
features. Winter dress resembles immatures but is less contrasting and more
yellowish grey. Unusually, it is the male, smaller and with more subdued colouring,
who sits on the eggs and cares for the young. Completely unafraid, he often jumps
up like a lemming, a yard or so from the observer's feet. The brighter female leads
courtship and mating displays. Like the ringed plover, she performs a courtship flight
while emitting rhythmical bright 'vit-i-vih' cries which she also uses when disturbed.
Other notes are a bright tinkling 'plitt' and, when taking to the wing, a dunlin-like
'kurr'. The dotterel breeds on dry mountain heaths, often on small elevated plateaux
in the lichen zone, and, exceptionally, at lower altitudes. It occurs locally and in
small numbers. In spring, small groups will pause along river valleys and low-lying
places, waiting for the snows to melt higher in the mountains. The diet is mainly
insects and their larvae.

Golden plover   *Pluvialis apricaria*   27 cm

A common and characteristic feature of open moorland, most often near marshier
areas and peat bogs in wooded country. Both the male and female look after the
brood, and when disturbed they produce a persistent heart-rending 'eeah'. The
summoning calls are a soft 'pee' and 'puh'. From the mountain can also be heard
a melancholy plaintive 'plu-i-vie' which is rhythmically repeated during the courtship flight, alternating with a slightly drier, rolling 'prre-quirrio, prre-quirrio'. In
flight the colour of the upper parts and white bars on the wings immediately
distinguish this bird from the dotterel. The female usually has less black on her face
and belly than the male. Immatures are completely speckled in grey, green and white,
but with a paler belly. The golden plover is numerous in the mountains, and
migrating flocks rest on grassland and along shorelines where they feed on seeds.

Ringed plover

Dotterel

Golden plover

juvenile

Dotterel

Golden plover

Temminck's stint

Purple sandpiper   *Calidris maritima*   23 cm

This dull grey bird with a smattering of bronze yellow and rust might be expected to breed in the very highest boulder and lichen country. And so it does, particularly on stony plateaux close to small lakes. Along the Arctic coasts it nests at lower altitudes, and in Iceland at sea-level, but conditions on its nesting grounds in the mountains usually exclude other waders. The winter plumage is completely grey with a shimmer of brownish purple, and the legs are orange. Many nesting birds seem to have no more than a trace or two of summer plumage. Outside the nesting season the purple sandpiper frequents rocky coasts. It is usually unafraid when its eggs and young are close by, and runs in circles around an intruder, neck outstretched, emitting a sharp 'keutt' or, when very agitated, a soft gurgling 'kruhuhuhuhu'. The flight call is a trickling – and usually nasal – 'keutt' or 'kveeut'. During the courtship flight there are long sequences of notes like the dunlin's, although of a more nasal timbre, including a prolonged rumbling 'kreuvirrr' and 'hurr-i'. Feeds on insects, small molluscs, shrimps, seeds and the green parts of plants.

Temminck's stint   *Calidris temminckii*   15 cm

Easily recognized because it is so small. The tundra in Norway's extreme north and further east is also the breeding ground of the little stint (*C. minuta*) 14 cm, but that species has black legs and a pronounced reddish tinge to its upper parts. Temminck's stint is fond of muddy or sandy beaches with some vegetation, and it breeds fairly commonly beside rivers, river deltas and lakesides where there are birch and willow. Along the Arctic coast it occurs commonly beside small freshwater pools, often close to human settlements. The male has a pleasing courtship flight, hovering like a lark with his wings vibrating in a perfect V and calling with a delicate bell-like note. He often lands on top of a willow or on a fence post. Both sexes have a ringing 'tirr' in flight. Summer plumage varies, as in the case of the purple sandpiper. Immatures have uniformly grey-fawn upper parts with a pattern of pale-edged dark scaly feathers. The diet is mainly insects and other aquatic creatures.

Purple sandpiper

Temminck's stint

Purple sandpiper

Temminck's stint

Dunlin   *Calidris alpina*   17–20 cm

Breeds on grassy and sedge-grown coastal marshes and moorlands even above the
tree line. Easily recognized by its black belly and the bright rust of its upper parts.
The male performs a courtship flight with wings vibrating. Often quite a difficult
bird to spot, it has a buzzing trill which varies in tempo but is basically 'kruu, krru,
krru, krri, krri, krri, ru, ru, ru . . .' Its flight call is a rough rolling 'krrri' or 'chrrruit'.
The majority of dunlins overwintering along the coasts of Europe come from the
Siberian tundras. They feed mainly on small invertebrates.

Broad-billed sandpiper   *Limicola falcinellus*   17 cm

Breeds in the middle of extensive marshlands with sedge-grown quagmires. Its main
breeding area is in the coniferous zone, but it also occurs higher up towards the
birch zone, especially north of the 68th parallel where birch predominates in forest
areas even at lower altitudes. It can most often be observed during its striking courtship in the few twilight hours, when it flies to and fro, sometimes at quite a
considerable height, stopping dead every now and then to hover with its wings
uplifted and vibrating. At these times it makes a mechanical buzzing 'suirr suirr
suirr . . .' occasionally interpolated with a faster whirring 'suirrirrirrirr . . .' The flight
call is a buzzing 'chrryit'. A variation of this call is used when the bird is agitated.
The broad-billed sandpiper migrates towards the southeast and is then seen only
rarely in western Europe. Its fresh summer plumage has a fairly pale 'floury' look,
but by July or August wear and tear have made it much darker. Immatures seen
during the autumn migration in August–September are paler, more regularly
patterned, and the markings on their underparts are less distinct and confined to the
sides of the breast. In all plumages the two pale bars over the crown can make
identification positive, as do the muddy grey-brownish legs which are paler than
those of young dunlins. Insects and other small creatures make up most of the diet
during the summer.

Dunlin

Broad-billed sandpiper

juvenile

Dunlin

summer

summer

Broad-billed sandpiper

spring

Ruff *Philomachus pugnax* ♂30 cm ♀24 cm

Breeds in large numbers in lush grassy meadows and marshes in the north, from sea-level to the willow zone, but less commonly in the south. The males (ruffs) arrive first, congregating at the beginning of May. Their spectacular display ritual is performed in special places, often the same one each year, on a slightly drier ridge or mound. The colours of the 'ruff' of neck feathers seem to be endlessly varied. Their 'tournament' is a silent, hectic and impulsive display, with bowings, wing flutterings and aerial jumps. Each ruff defends his particular 'pitch' against all comers, but those with white collars seem to be able to move as they please. Towards midsummer they lose their plumes and go into a nondescript greyish fawn and white winter dress before migrating south. Consequently the females (reeves) are often seen alone later in the summer. When taking to the wing they are usually silent, but sometimes emit a low 'too-ee'. The flight is an awkward puppy-like flopping, showing a white wing bar and two white oval patches on the rump. Immatures resemble the reeve but have scaly markings with greyish fawn to red ochre margins against a dark background. Insects and other invertebrates, seeds and parts of plants are the birds' diet.

Redshank   *Tringa totanus*   28 cm

Locally common in birch and willow zones in the north, but not usually found in forest marshes. Breeds in meadows close to lakes, small ponds and flowing water, and, in the south, on coastal marshes. Easily recognized by its bright red legs, conspicuous white rump and trailing edge of the wing. Northern Scandinavian and Icelandic redshanks usually seem to be darker than those further south. The flight call is a soft whistling 'tyu-hu'. Near its nesting ground intruders are pursued with a persistent, even, hammering 'klee-klee-klee ...' The courtship flight is an undulating course with wings vibrating at the peak and held rigid into the trough, all the while emitting a 'choo-choo-choo' at varying speeds. Immatures have fawn pink to orange red legs, a brownish-fawn bill, brownish-grey upper parts speckled with fawn, striated sides to the breast and a white belly.

Greenshank   *Tringa nebularia*   30–35 cm

Occurs on open marshes and beside rivers up to the willow zone. Nests on drier ground, such as patches of sandy heath with pines, or on a nearby slope. This is why it can sometimes suddenly appear in a birch forest or on an exposed mountain, away from water. The long springy wings and oblong body shape are striking, but the legs are often retracted in flight. The flight call is a variable, deep, sighing 'two-two-two' and an agitated bird will emit a cracked 'kruipp-kruipp-kruipp'. The warning note is a persistent 'kyukyukyu ...' The courtship flight, like the redshank's, is a sighing, resounding, sometimes diver-like 'kluvi-kluvi ...', mostly at night.

Spotted redshank   *Tringa erythropus*   32 cm

The breeding plumage differs from other waders. It breeds on large tree-fringed sedge or grass marshes in the far north. It announces itself with a snappy but full-toned whistle, 'chuitt', followed after a short pause by another 'chuitt'. Soon after-wards a compact cigar-shaped bird shoots past at tremendous speed and disappears with wings held steeply downwards and with the flash of a broad white streak across its rump. During a short period near midsummer, in the few hours of twilight around midnight, the courtship ceremony is heard – an endless 'krrruh-iukrrruh-i-krrruh-i ...' with a magical buzzing sound. The immature's legs and bill are paler orange red, the upper parts sooty brown with pale patches, and the pale underparts have dense dark spots.

Redshank

Greenshank

Spotted redshank

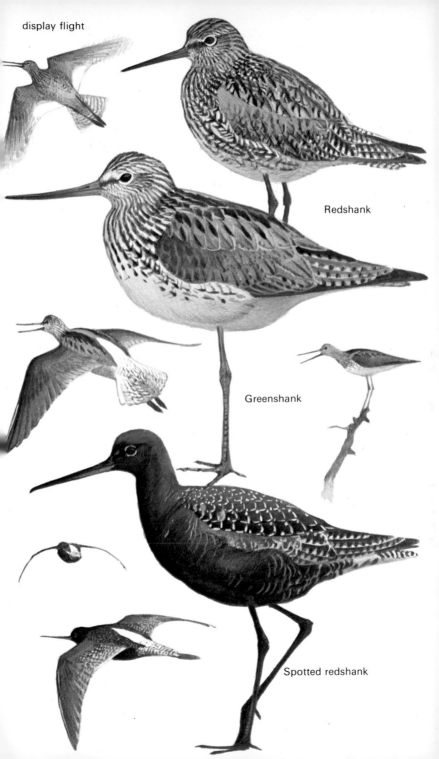

display flight

Redshank

Greenshank

Spotted redshank

Wood sandpiper   *Tringa glareola*   21 cm

A resident of sedge or grass-grown marshes with scattered pine trees or willows. It is unimpressive in appearance with a greyish speckled look about it, but its smaller size, moss-green legs and boldness are differences from its larger relatives. A noisy bird, its courtship song is persistent during spring and early summer, with a yodelling 'liltie-liltie-liltie' and, during courtship display, a mechanically clattering 'yayaya'. When its young have hatched the wood sandpiper uses a persistent 'kipp-kipp-kipp . . .' warning note. It hovers with wings shaking and barks above an intruder's head, an added hazard while finding one's way through treacherous marshland quagmires. The flight call is a pleasant whistling 'chiff-iff-iff'.

Common sandpiper   *Tringa hypoleucos*   20 cm

Common over much of Europe, and one of the most widespread waders beside clear lakes, rivers and on river banks from the lowlands into the birch zone. The courtship song is a rapid sequence of needle-sharp 'pipitividih-pipitividih . . .' A more agitated version is heard, together with a penetrating 'hiip', when the bird is disturbed. The flight call on take-off is an equally bright and sharp 'hee-dee-dee'. The flight is very characteristic – alternating glides on stiffly downturned wings and bouts of vibrating wing beats. When perched on a stone or a stump it bobs its tail almost continuously.

Red-necked phalarope   *Phalaropus lobatus*   18 cm

Breeds on small grass-fringed tarns and marshy waters. Common and amazingly tame, with a neat profile. This buoyant swimmer rapidly and mechanically nods its way across the water, snapping left and right at mosquitoes and other small insects as it goes. Sometimes it spins on one spot like a clockwork toy, generating a vortex which whirls up all kinds of small creatures that are snapped up with lightning speed. The calls are many and varied, but a woodpecker-like or pebble-crunching tone is typical, 'kirrik' or 'kitt'. There are also a fast 'check', a hard 'krreu' and a protracted, snipe-like, hissing 'weesp'. The female's colour is brighter – she attends to courtship and the mating ritual, while the male takes care of the eggs and young. Relatively small numbers migrate past the coasts of northern Europe on their way to wintering areas well out in tropical seas.

Wood sandpiper

Common sandpiper

Red-necked phalarope

Wood sandpiper

Common sandpiper

Juvenile

Red-necked
phalarope

♀

♂

Whimbrel   Bar-tailed godwit ♂

Bar-tailed godwit   *Limosa lapponica*   33–42 cm

Breeds in the tundra and from the northern boundary of the conifer zone in swamps and waterlogged moorland with mossy tussocks and dwarf birch. Seen in larger numbers when migrating to and from its winter habitats on the central mudflats of western Europe and, in summer, along the Arctic coast of northern Europe. The immature bird's plumage resembles the curlew's. Its nasal calls have a dark tone with a rapid 'view-view' or 'ved-ved-ved-ved' in flight. The mating call is a series of churning verses, similar in tone but delivered at varying speed: 'keuvah, keuvah, keuvah …' When disturbed it utters a persistent raucous 'kaka, kaka, kaka …' at a tempo which depends on exactly how perturbed it happens to be. Lives on insects, worms, molluscs and berries.

Whimbrel   *Numenius phaeopus*   43–47 cm

A small curlew seen in remote northern Europe on a mountain heath, highland fen or thin forest of mountain birch along a river or shoreline is certainly a whimbrel. In the east, and on some Atlantic islands, it also breeds relatively far south, and here one also finds the curlew (*N. arquata*) 56–63 cm in cultivated fens and meadows. The whimbrel, however, is smaller and rounder, with a darker mantle and wings, and has snipe-like markings on its crown. When concerned for its eggs or young it often settles on a nearby stone, fence or dead tree and gives a jerky 'che-ke-ke-ke-ke'. Its contact call is a laughing bubbling trill often of seven syllables, 'pu-pu-hu-hu-hu-hu-hu'. The courtship flight and song resemble the curlew's – the song a slow crooning which accelerates and changes into a prolonged rolling trill – but the tone is gentler and 'earthier' than the curlew's. Feeds on invertebrates and berries.

Bar-tailed godwit

Whimbrel

Bar-tailed godwit

Whimbrel

Great snipe *Gallinago media* 29 cm

Common over much of northern Europe a hundred years ago, but now a rare breeding bird of waterlogged mountain slopes and drier fenland with willows. The great snipe is very bold and waits until the observer is only a few metres away before taking to the wing. It then flies in complete silence or with a few hoarse protracted notes, 'etch-etch-etch'. It does not zig-zag on take-off, and the straight flight ends rather abruptly with a 'pancake' landing in the vegetation about twenty or thirty metres away. Differs from the snipe in flight by greater weight, rounder body and wing shape (more like the woodcock), slower flight, more conspicuous markings on its underparts, white outer tail feathers and two distinct white bars outlining the darker greater coverts. On their breeding grounds the males form groups for the courtship rituals on tussocks in the osier thickets. Their chromatic twittering notes, like a symphony of icicles, are followed by a wooden clattering of bills leading to a soft buzzing. Note also the white tail feathers which shine brilliantly when displayed in the faint light, and the short flights and grouse-like leaps accompanied by a faint wing noise. A migrant to the southeast, it is rare in western Europe.

Snipe *Gallinago gallinago* 27 cm

Well-known and common in most sedge or grass-grown swamps, fens or water-meadows from sea-level and deep into the willow zone. The aerial courtship ritual includes ascents accompanied by a drumming as the outer tail feathers vibrate in a steep dive. Perched on a vantage point, it also produces a loud, rhythmically ticking 'tick-a, tick-a, tick-a ... (chuck-a)', sometimes changing to 6/8 time. When rising it casts about nervously, uttering one or two hoarse 'ketch' notes.

Jack snipe *Lymnocryptes minimus* 20 cm

A rare breeding bird in wet swamps with sedges and cotton-grass, in thinly wooded areas and in the tundra. The courtship flight resembles the snipe's, but the displaying bird is even harder to locate; high up in the twilight sky there is a very distinctive dull 'kock-oa-kock-oa-kock-oa...' like the distant sound of a galloping horse. On the ground it sits very still until the observer comes within a metre or so. At take-off, rather slowly compared with the snipe, there is time to observe the short bill, stiff-necked, upward-pointing posture, triangular head and pointed tail on a rather truncated rear. It usually lands again almost immediately.

Great snipe

Snipe

Jack snipe

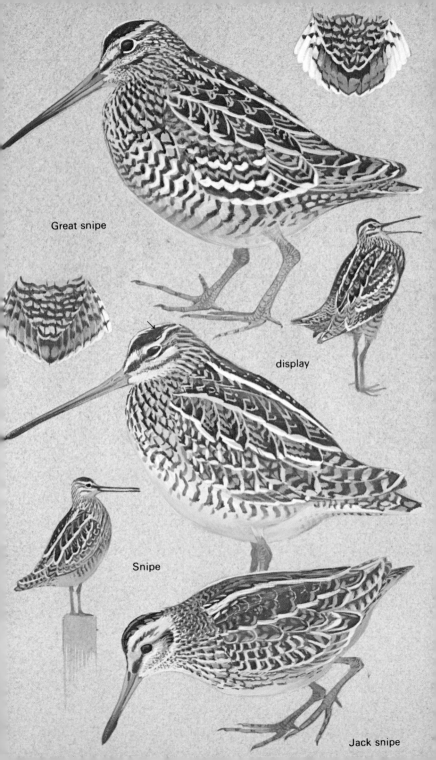

Great snipe

display

Snipe

Jack snipe

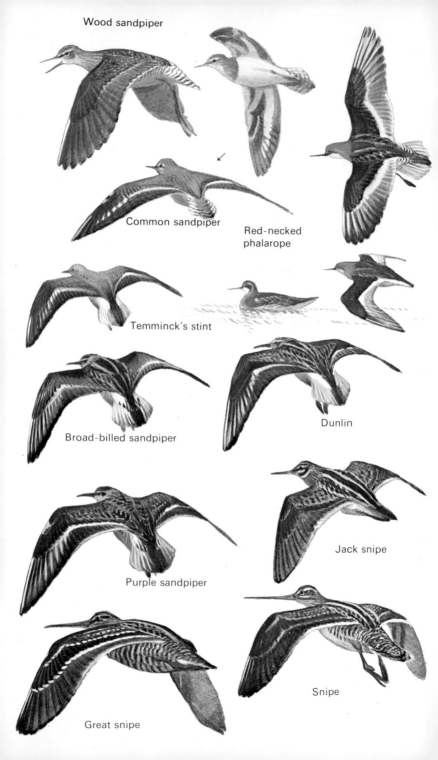

Wood sandpiper

Common sandpiper

Red-necked phalarope

Temminck's stint

Broad-billed sandpiper

Dunlin

Purple sandpiper

Jack snipe

Great snipe

Snipe

juvenile

juvenile

Long-tailed skua

Long-tailed skua *Stercorarius longicaudus*

51–60 cm
including 13–25 cm
tail projection

A mountain and tundra species that prefers feeding on lemmings and other rodents in the nesting season. Numbers fluctuate considerably from year to year: it is common when rodents are abundant, while in other years it can be almost completely absent. Breeds above the tree line. Although not particularly attracted to or dependent on water, it sometimes – especially in a bad year for rodents – heads for the shores of mountain lakes to catch insects. It is relatively unafraid, and the slender tern-like silhouette and fast easy flight are a pleasure to behold. On the Arctic coasts confusion is possible with the light phase of the Arctic skua (*S. parasiticus*). The Arctic, however, is slightly larger and heavier, with a much shorter tail projection, less brownish black, a sharply delineated cap and a considerably larger pale patch on the underside of the primaries. The long-tailed's calls are a snappy 'kiu' or 'kiew', a rather buzzard-like 'piaa' and a warning cry of single or repeated short hard 'kriepp' sounds. It winters out to sea, and is much less often seen on migration than its larger relatives. (See distribution map p. 78.)

77

Common gulls mobbing a rough-legged buzzard

Common gull *Larus canus* 41–45 cm

Common in mountain areas with clear lakes where, together with the Arctic tern, it is often the only gull or tern species to be seen. The black-headed gull (*L. ridibundus*), with a chocolate-colour cap, has rapidly spread to the north, however, and is regularly observed close to the Arctic coast. The herring gull (*L. argentatus*), also encountered along the coast and on lakes at lower altitudes, is larger than the common gull, with a thicker bill and a yellow iris. Common gulls breed in small colonies, mainly on small islands or peninsulas in a lake. High in the mountains they often move in before the ice melts and the couple, settling immediately on a bare tussock or mound, stand out like snowballs. Their somewhat nasal, often shrill notes break the silence around many a lake, and they are particularly noisy when squabbling over a dead fish or food scraps discarded by hikers. They usually chase predators with a persistent chorus of 'gliu-gliu-gliu ...' Their food ranges from small insects and worms to voles. Year-olds rarely visit mountain lakes but are commonly seen along coasts and, inland, further south. They have a grey mantle, but retain the immature wing markings which by now are pale and faded.

Arctic tern *Sterna paradisaea* 36–42 cm

The summer route follows the icy waters of mountain and tundra as close to the North Pole as there is snow-free ground. It is fairly common along rivers and, together with the common gull and common sandpiper, is often the prominent feature of mountain lakes and bare forest. It breeds far into the willow zone but is most numerous along the sea coasts, especially in Iceland where immense colonies may number more than 100,000 pairs. The common tern (*S. hirundo*) does not occur in Iceland, the Faeroes or in the mountains or tundra but breeds by the sea as far north as the Varanger Peninsula. In the late summer migration to the oceans of the southern hemisphere, some birds actually reach the Antarctic.

Long-tailed skua   Common gull   Arctic tern

juvenile

Common gull

Arctic tern

Eagle owl

Owls   Order *Strigiformes*

The thirteen European owl species are divided into two families, *Tytonidae* (barn owl) and *Strigidae*, which contains the other twelve. All are active in the dark, to a greater or lesser extent, and thus their night vision is very well developed. In some species the sense of hearing also plays a crucial part in locating prey. The ear apertures lie behind the stiff feathers of the facial disc which focuses sound into them and is probably the main distinguishing characteristic of an owl. The eyes are specially constructed to register the meagre nocturnal light. The retina consists almost entirely of light-sensitive rods with hardly any cones, which makes for good night vision but a poor sense of colour. Also, the rods are grouped close together to capture very small amounts of light. This capacity for collecting light is further improved by special features such as the thick lens and tubular rather than spherical shape of the eye. Small rodents, mostly active at night, are especially hunted by many owl species, whose very soft plumage reduces the wing noise that could warn an intended victim.

Snowy owl

Snowy owl

♂ during display

♀

Snowy owl *Nyctea scandiaca* 61 cm

Breeds on moorland and tundra. Successful breeding depends on large populations of lemmings or other rodents. It wanders throughout the Arctic areas of the northern hemisphere, settling where food is plentiful, but occurs irregularly in northern Europe, and in some years is not seen at all. Occasional individuals winter on moorland and open farmland further south in Europe. The male, smaller than the female, has few, if any, dark patches, while immatures are more heavily marked than the female. The snowy owl is a surprisingly good flier, with longer and more pointed wings than most other owls. The territorial call is a short, deep trumpeting 'goh' repeated at intervals of a few seconds, while the warning note is a hoarse 'kva kva kva ...', varied in tempo and pitch, that resembles the raven's. The nest is often built on a low hillock or ridge. The grass around it is conspicuously green and thick because it is manured with droppings and the remnants of prey.

Hawk owl *Surnia ulula* 38 cm

Most often seen in clearings, firebreaks, power line rides or similar open spaces in the forest zone and, more commonly, in sparse open woodland at the tree line. The nesting places are in hollow trees or occasionally in abandoned crows' nests. It lives on rodents, especially voles, and the number of pairs breeding in a given area fluctuates considerably from year to year. Odd birds may occasionally be seen far outside the normal range. It is active in the daytime and often perches like a big fat great grey shrike on top of a dead tree or telegraph pole so that it is more frequently spotted than other owls. In flight it resembles a big sparrow hawk, with its long tail and small relatively pointed wings and fast shallow wing beats. The territorial call, mainly heard at night, is a protracted chattering or bubbling trill 'prullullullu ...' The female replies with a hoarse, rather querulous 'kschu-lipp'. The warning call near the nest is a jerky sequence of 'ke(ke)-ke-ke-ke ...' or 'keu-keu ...', loud and harsh, not unlike a kestrel.

Short-eared owl *Asio flammeus* 37 cm

A bird of marshes, heaths, moorland and rough grassland. Although active during the day, in northern areas it is most often seen hunting during the twilight hours. Because voles are the main diet, numbers fluctuate widely from year to year. Jerky wing movements make the flight look rather mechanical, but the glides are rapid and elegant. Many Arctic individuals are very pale, sometimes almost a dingy white, and from a distance they can be taken for young herring gulls with faded plumage. The male's territorial call is a soft thumping 'do-do-do-do-do', mostly heard during the courtship flight when he circles slowly to a great height. There is also a short series of wing claps.

Hawk owl

Short-eared owl

82–83

Hawk owl

Short-eared owl

Pygmy owl

Pygmy owl   *Glaucidium passerinum*   17 cm

Breeds, occasionally commonly, in the conifer zone and is usually encountered where the forest borders swamps or glades. It announces itself with a rhythmically repeated whistling 'piuh' (nearly 'piuk') somewhat like the bullfinch. It will whistle when perched, preferably in the top of a spruce tree, and particularly at dawn and dusk, often wagging its tail. In autumn the bird emits a fast, slightly jerky sequence of bright whistlings with a rise in pitch towards the end, 'chut, chut, chut, chit, chit'. Active in the daytime, the flight over open country resembles the woodpecker's, with a series of fast wing beats followed by a deeply scooping glide. In addition to a diet of rodents there is a ceaseless hunt for small birds, which loudly warn each other of its approach. In winter some pygmy owls move to deciduous woodland or around farms where there is a good supply of these small birds. Prey is stored in holes in trees and elsewhere and it nests in abandoned woodpecker nest-holes.

Tengmalm's owl   *Aegolius funereus*   26 cm

Depending on the supply of rodents, it breeds commonly some years in certain areas and sparsely in others. The nests are made in holes abandoned by black woodpeckers so the bird is therefore commonest in mature coniferous forests with a mixture of tall deciduous trees. It will also use nestboxes. Occasionally takes small birds up to the size of a thrush. In some years large numbers emigrate, thus it is possible to make an identification far beyond the normal distribution area. The male's courtship is most intensive during winter and spring, less so in autumn, and takes place only at night. The courtship or territorial call is a fast vibrant sequence of hollow staccato barks, 'po-po-po-po-po'. These vary in length and tone from one male to another but are repeated at intervals of a few seconds over long periods. When disturbed, Tengmalm's owl produces a nasal 'kuweuk' and a hard 'kipp'. It is difficult to spot because it is mostly a night bird. In daytime it sits immobile in a thick spruce tree, but is not at all shy of humans. The young are in a chocolate-brown dress when they leave the nest, and beg for food with a hoarse whistling 'karii'.

Pygmy owl

Tengmalm's owl

84–85

Pygmy owl

uvenile

Tengmalm's owl

Ural owl   *Strix uralensis*   61 cm

Nests sparsely in old coniferous and mixed forest in central Europe and also in unmixed Alpine beech woods. Rodents (particularly voles), caught in clearings, are the main diet. The population fluctuates less drastically than other birds specializing in rodents, which suggests that a deficiency of rodents can be made up by hunting hazel hen, black grouse and jay. Nests are constructed in hollow dead trees, nest-boxes or, more rarely, in bulky old twig nests. It looks like an overgrown tawny owl, but seems very pale, with black eyes. The male bird's territorial call, a soft hooting 'voho ... voho-hovoho', slightly vibrates in the last three syllables and is audible from more than a kilometre. Only solitary males maintain the song for any length of time. Settled pairs are relatively quiet: the male announces his approach with food and the female responds with a raucous barking 'weuv'. During the mating season both sexes also produce a sequence of deep trumpeting notes, 'wowowowowo' with a slight acceleration towards the end. The female's note is brighter. The female's warning call is a short canine bark, 'waff' or 'waff-aff', which is lower and softer from the male. The young beg for food with a hissing 'pchiepp'.

Great grey owl   *Strix nebulosa*   69 cm

Found in the taiga in coniferous and mixed forest with fields, swamps or similar open spaces. The numbers depend entirely on the supply of rodents: in some years the bird is quite common locally, while in others it seems to emigrate and is nowhere to be seen. Eggs are laid in large nests of twigs that have been abandoned by other birds. Sits on a tree or pole, usually between one and four metres off the ground, while listening or looking for voles. In summer it hunts all day and night. During the steady and well-balanced flight with long glides note the wide dark bar on the long tail, two pale patches on the wide wings and the large head. The male's territorial call is only heard during the darkest hours and never carries more than about 400 m. The soft note is hard to locate but the volume always seems to be the same, irrespective of distance, and the tone is rather like the call of the bittern. Usually it consists of ten or twelve hoots, emitted slowly but accelerating, and then losing some volume towards the end. The full sequence takes six or seven seconds but an agitated male's is about twice this speed. The female answers with a high-pitched and remarkably gentle 'cheh cheh cheh'. She also has a loud cracked trill (the young have a similar begging call) and a faint whining 'choh' or a more insistent 'koyoh' combined with a low cooing. When an intruder approaches the nest, the pair clap their bills and give a dull hoarse 'hoch-hoch-hoch' to warn him off. An agitated female's high-pitched scream sounds like a pig during slaughter.

Ural owl

Great grey owl

Ural owl

Great grey owl

Great grey owl

Hawk owl

Ural owl

Short-eared owl

Snowy owl

Tengmalm's owl

Pygmy owl

fledglings

Hawk owl

Ural owl

Great grey owl

Black woodpecker ♂

Three-toed woodpecker on ringed spruce trunk

Woodpeckers *Picidae*

Apart from the species included here, the black woodpecker, great spotted wood-pecker and wryneck occur sparsely to fairly commonly in mixed or coniferous forests of large trees up to the birch zone. The grey-headed and white-backed woodpeckers are also found in southern areas of the conifer zone.

Lesser spotted woodpecker *Dendrocopos minor* 14.5 cm

Occurs sparsely in hardwood and mixed forest well into the birch zone. Its smaller size makes it immediately distinguishable from other woodpeckers as well as the female's lack of red on her crown. The note is a snappy perky 'kick' and a rather sluggish repetitive 'ki-ki-ki-ki-ki-ki-ki' like the wryneck's. The weak drumming, about one second, is usually performed twice in rapid succession with a short interval.

Three-toed woodpecker *Picoides tridactylus* 22 cm

Fairly common in mature spruce and mountain birch forests. The 'kick' note is 'wetter' and softer than the great spotted woodpecker's, but its 'kuck' varies. This bird drums constantly in late winter and spring: a tentative start which gathers strength and continues evenly and distinctly for more than one second. Feeds mainly on beetles and other insects and their larvae found under the bark of the lower parts of dead and half-dead spruce trees. The feeding behaviour of males and females differs, mainly in winter; the male, with a stouter bill, attacks thicker trunks and branches which makes it possible for the species to occupy a wider niche in its habitat. This aids survival because there is virtually no competition from other woodpecker species in northern spruce forests.

Lesser spotted woodpecker

Three-toed woodpecker

Lesser spotted woodpecker ♂

♂

Three-toed woodpecker ♀

Perching birds   Order *Passeriformes*

This very extensive order contains more species and individuals than any other, but they vary a great deal in size and habits. Most of the species included here breed exclusively in the area covered by this volume, but many which are common in central Europe are also found in the north – in wooded areas and near human settlements. Thus birdwatchers may frequently observe sand martin, house martin, skylark, crow, magpie, starling, great tit, house sparrow, tree sparrow, siskin and bullfinch. Some of these are described on pp. 98–100. It is useful, when trying to identify an unfamiliar bird, to be able to link it to a family. The following families are represented in Europe.

Larks (*Alaudidae*) are camouflaged and heavily-built ground birds with stout bills. **Swallows** (*Hirundinidae*) are skilful fliers and live on insects caught on the wing. The slender, long-legged **wagtails** and **pipits** (*Motacillidae*) have an elegant posture and a relatively long tail. **Shrikes** (*Laniidae*) are represented by the great grey shrike, with a stout, hooked, predatory bill. Outwardly similar **starlings** (*Sturnidae*) and **waxwings** (*Bombycillidae*) differ in colour, food habits and behaviour. The thick-billed, mostly omnivorous, **crows** (*Corvidae*), the largest of the perching species, are mainly marked in black, grey and white. **Dippers** (*Cinclidae*) are semi-aquatic. The small brown **wrens** (*Troglodytidae*) have a short upturned tail. The large group of **accentors** (*Prunellidae*) and **warblers** (*Sylviidae*) are small and mostly insectivorous with nondescript markings. They move quickly and are best identified by their song. **Flycatchers** (*Muscicapidae*), with an upright posture, capture insects in mid-air. **Thrushes** (*Turdidae*), a large group with a 'perky' stance, include thrushes, wheatear, whinchat, red-flanked bluetail, bluethroat and robin. The **bearded reedling** (*Timaliidae*) and **penduline tit** (*Remizidae*) are not found in the area. **Tits** (*Paridae*) are forest and garden dwellers. The great, crested, and coal tits breed in the area, as does the long-tailed tit to some extent. Of the **nuthatches** (*Sittidae*), **treecreepers** (*Certhiidae*) and **sparrows** (*Ploceidae*), the two northern European representatives are the house sparrow and tree sparrow which occur locally within the area. For **finches** (*Fringillidae*) and **buntings** (*Emberizidae*), see p. 115.

Citrine wagtail   *Motacilla citreola*   18 cm

Breeds in marshes and meadows in extreme northeastern Europe, both in the tundra from the Kanin Peninsula eastwards, and also in the central USSR, in a wide belt extending eastwards from the Volga. Has nested once in Scotland and once in Sweden, but otherwise occurs only very rarely in western Europe during spring and autumn. Autumn observations are almost entirely limited to young birds in their first winter plumage, which differ from young yellow wagtails (first winter females) in that they do not have yellow on their underparts. They have grey flanks, often with a touch of brownish-grey upper parts (never olive shades), distinct, pale, wide superciliaries, and a slightly longer tail with a grey to greyish-black rump. One note resembles the yellow wagtail's 'zieee' during migration but is shorter and sharper and combined with an 'r' to give 'srriep'.

Various types of perching birds at rest, with feathers slightly ruffled. Top row, left to right: meadow pipit, redstart ♀ and brambling ♀ in winter. Bottom row, left to right: willow warbler. Siberian tit and reed bunting ♀.

Citrine wagtail ♂

♂ thunbergi autumn

juvenile ♀ autumn

Yellow wagtail

autumn

Citrine wagtail

juvenile

Shore lark   *Eremophila alpestris*   16.5 cm

A scarce breeding bird of open mountain country, mostly on dry, stony plateaux or gravel ridges just above the willow zone. Along the Arctic coast it also breeds on stony beaches. The distinctive head marking makes it easy to recognize, but it is shy and often creeps behind stones and small mounds. It usually attracts by its note when disturbed, a variable 'piih', sometimes a 'piu', very like the note of the snow bunting. The high-pitched, short, snappy bi- or trisyllabic flight note is 'tsee-toe-tsee' or 'tse-tsee'. The song, also similar to the snow bunting's in tone, is a short ragged verse sometimes repeated to form a more sustained lark-like twitter. Insects, seeds and other vegetable matter are its diet.

Yellow wagtail   *Motacilla flava*   16.5 cm

Breeds commonly in swamps, damp meadows and marshes, alongside streams and lake shores up to the willow zone. There are several European races, each with a slightly different plumage. The white wagtail (*M. alba*) which breeds in many habitats, often close to water or at a considerable altitude, is black, white and grey. Immature yellow wagtails have yellow-fawn, grey and brown markings and a band of dark patches across the breast. In some races occasional females have grey and white markings. Mountain walkers often come across the yellow wagtail perched in the top of a stunted bush or birch. The variety of calls are a pleasing 'zieh' or 'zrrie' as well as a short 'psit' and a bright dunnock-like 'zi-si-si'. The song is a continuous twittering version of the call. The flight is deeply undulating. Lives mainly on insects.

Shore lark

Yellow wagtail

Shore lark

Yellow wagtail

Red-throated pipit   *Anthus cervinus*   14.5 cm

Breeds in small numbers in the Scandinavian mountain range but more commonly towards the Arctic coast in open grasslands or marshes with osier bushes. The amount of red on the throat and breast varies a great deal. The red-throated is distinguished from the meadow pipit by its note and by the heavier, more contrasting markings on its back, rump and sides. In autumn it is more heavily striated than the meadow pipit, on a bright brownish-red ground – no suggestion of olive green – with more distinct white wing bars and a thin white ring around the eye. The song resembles the meadow pipit's but is more fiery, in shorter stanzas. The call may be woven in – two or three prolonged, bright and somewhat hoarse 'spiiih'. Other notes are a disyllabic rolling 'churrpp' and the warning call, a reiterated 'chu' or a softer 'stuh'. Rare in western Europe during autumn migration.

Meadow pipit   *Anthus pratensis*   14.5 cm

Because the different pipit species may be difficult to identify, their calls are the best guide. These three northern species, however, have somewhat different nesting habitats. The meadow pipit favours dry, open mountain heaths down to the birch forest and on moorland at lower altitudes. The damp osier marshes above the conifer line are the habitat of the red-throated pipit, while the tree pipit prefers areas towards the conifers and the deciduous tree zone. The meadow pipit's song flight first rises and then 'parachutes' down. Its song opens with fast accelerating 'tsip's' followed by protracted 'tsuht' or 'siu' notes which end with a bright trill. The warning call, a persistent 'stitt-itt', is heard by mountain trekkers during high summer, as is the food-begging call of the young, a discordant 'stih'. Particularly when agitated, this bird, like the tree pipit, often heads for the tops of tall bushes and dead trees. Mainly an insect-eater, it winters on marshes and grassy farmland.

Tree pipit   *Anthus trivialis*   15 cm

A characteristic bird of wooded country, often common in the north, especially in more open dry woodland. It is usually the song that attracts attention. The song flight resembles the meadow pipit's, but starts from a tree top. The song is also somewhat similar to the meadow pipit's but is more variable and tuneful, with a chaffinch-like introduction. The warning call is a regularly repeated 'stutt', and the flight note a hoarse 'pizzt' or 'buzzt' and a 'psit' resembling the meadow pipit's.

Red-throated pipit

Meadow pipit

Tree pipit

Red-throated pipit

Meadow pipit

Tree pipit

Waxwings in a mountain ash

Great grey shrike *Lanius excubitor* 24 cm

A big, pale, grey, black and white bird which most often perches upright on top of a tree or bush. It is a rare breeding bird in our area, choosing open places such as clearings, river banks or moorland margins. It searches for rodents, small birds and insects from strategic look-out points or by hovering like a kestrel. Surplus food is impaled on thorns as a reserve for less successful hunting days. A fairly quiet bird on the whole, it sometimes sings – or, rather, recites – various notes, which include vibrant trills and squeaks, often with various confusing sections of mimicry. In flight it has a brightly rolling 'shrrree' and a prolonged nasal 'eeeh', slightly reminiscent of the jay.

Waxwing *Bombycilla garrulus* 19 cm

Breeds irregularly and in small numbers in the northernmost areas of coniferous forest, mostly in old forest where there is plenty of lichen and a sprinkling of deciduous trees with undergrowth that yields a generous berry supply. The observer can quickly identify a waxwing at close quarters but it is a shy bird, most often seen as it sweeps past above the spruce trees. It then seems very much like a starling, but its flight is faster and more graceful and its profile more slender. Every now and then it gives a brightly ringing 'sirr'. It has a simple and unpretentious song. During the nesting season the diet is mainly flying insects caught with all the elegance of a bee-eater. Berries and fruit make up the bulk of the diet for the rest of the year. Flocks of waxwings migrate south in the late autumn and are seen in parks and gardens feasting on berries of rowan, white-beam, cotoneaster, rose hips and on any apples and pears that remain on the trees.

Great grey shrike

Waxwing

Great grey shrike

Waxwing

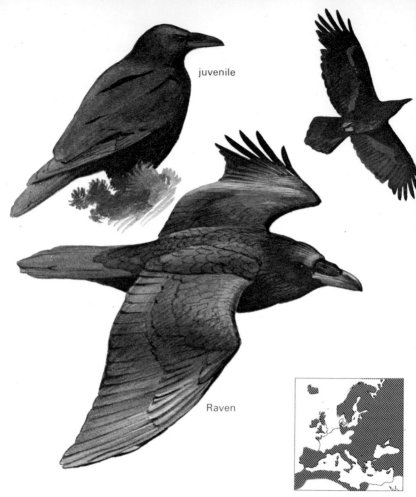

juvenile

Raven

Raven   *Corvus corax*   65 cm

Despite its limited numbers, the raven lends character to the mountains, especially in autumn and winter when most other species have migrated. The call, a deep metallic and slightly jarring 'krroap' that carries for an incredible distance, is often the first sign of its presence. During spring one can also hear a 'klong', as if someone a long distance away was banging on a metal cylinder, and a rapid 'klock' when the bird goes through its exciting aerobatic display ritual of looping the loop or plummeting towards the ground. Its warning call is a persistent unmusical 'arrk-arrk-arrk'. When seen on the wing the distinguishing characteristics are a wedge-shaped tail, thick head and neck and relatively narrow wing tips. It glides frequently with wings held out straight. The crow, which now breeds commonly as far as the tree line, is only half as big and has a rounded tail and blunter wings. The raven lives on carrion of all kinds – birds' eggs, nestlings and rodents.

Siberian jay

Siberian jay *Perisoreus infaustus* 28 cm

Small groups are residents of the dense northern spruce forests. The young fledge as early as June. Humans arouse their curiosity, and one by one they will glide over in deep undulations and then, quite suddenly, land very close to the observer. They often disappear with equal suddenness, but with their particularly warm and luxurious plumage and rust-coloured tails they are unlikely to be confused with other species. They may seem to be taciturn, but quite often produce many of the unfamiliar forest sounds such as buzzard-like mewings and jay-like screechings. Their several other imitative notes are relatively soft and subdued. Insects and various small creatures (including eggs and young of small birds), berries and seeds are often collected in the autumn and hidden in clefts in the bark of trees.

Dipper *Cinclus cinclus* 18 cm

Surprisingly widely distributed in Europe, the dipper nests beneath waterfalls and beside fast-flowing rivers and is therefore more common in mountainous and high-land areas. Although distinctive, it evades discovery by blending with the colours of the rushing water. However, the very sharp, slightly rasping 'stritts' note usually penetrates the noisy background. The song is a subdued, rather unsystematic combination of squeaking and twittering sequences. Most often the bird perches on a stone in the rapids, bobbing and turning rather impatiently. Its unusual weight, short stout wings and powerful legs and claws enable it to forage for insect larvae and molluscs. Northern birds migrate south, but go no further than to escape the ice. Immature dress is grey with scaly black markings and an indistinct pale bib.

102–103

Typical residents of mountain regions

Dunnock (*Prunella modularis*) 14.5 cm. A shy mountain bird that prefers thickets and bushes well into the birch region and seldom appears for more than a few moments at a time. There is a dark overall impression. Attracts attention by its song from the top of a bush or young spruce – a pleasant, high-pitched jingle.

Sedge warbler (*Acrocephalus schoenobaenus*) 13 cm. Locally common in northern mountain ranges along river valleys, and deltas with osiers and swamp vegetation. Sings hectically in the early summer nights from atop a bush and during short flights. The persistent song alternates between hoarse rasping notes, bright trills and much mimicry of other birds.

Whinchat (*Saxicola rubetra*) 12.5 cm. A distinctive short-tailed bird, common in fertile meadowlands from the coast well into the hay meadows of mountain valleys. The extremely variable song is often incoherent and capricious, basically a fast crunching twitter interspersed with skilful imitative sounds.

Spotted flycatcher (*Muscicapa striata*) 14 cm. Common in open, park-like wooded country, especially on sandy heaths. Breeds in the forest zone, often close to human settlement, and up to the birch forest line. Makes sudden sorties against flying insects, often returning to the same perch. The call is a delicate 'ptsirr' or 'tsii' and the poorly-formed song repeats the call and whistlings.

Pied flycatcher (*Ficedula hypoleuca*) 13 cm. Common to sparse in open hard-wood and mixed woodland deep into the mountain birch belt. Female markings are grey-brown where the male is black. The song is fast, perky and vibrant, full of various bright, ringing and scratchy sounds. The warning note is a persistent 'pick, pick, pick ...'

Redstart (*Phoenicurus phoenicurus*) 14 cm. Common in open forest country, parks, gardens and sandy pine-clad heaths. Sings at dawn from the top of a high tree, often a spruce. The melancholy song often includes imitative sounds, but with bright clear notes. It begins with a 'hyitt', followed by a rolling 'tui-tui-tui-tui ...' The summoning note is 'huit', and when the bird is agitated the note is 'huit-chuuck-chuuck ...'

Dipper

Dunnock

Sedge warbler

Whinchat

♀

♂

Spotted flycatcher

Pied flycatcher

♂

Redstart

♀

♂

Arctic warbler   *Phylloscopus borealis*   12 cm

Breeds very rarely and irregularly in northern Europe in stream gorges and on birch-covered mountain slopes. Slightly larger and more robust than the willow warbler, it has a conspicuously long and thick supercilium, a long bill and a short bright bar on its wing (sometimes, too, a second bar along the middle coverts), although this bar may wear away during the summer. Its song is a high-pitched trill. The call is a rapid 'tsvi-ipp' and a sharp 'tzri' or 'tzre' like the dipper's; these notes become harder and sharper when the bird is agitated. The nest does not have a feather lining. Winters in southeast Asia, returning about midsummer.

Willow warbler   *Phylloscopus trochilus*   11 cm

Common in mixed deciduous woods and very numerous in mountain birch woods and scrub, often nesting far into the willow zone. The tuneful, silvery, trickling song is a woodland feature of early summer. The populations nesting in the north are often very pale because they lack shades of yellow. The call is a soft 'whoo-eet' and there is also a 'ziet', probably used by pairs during mating ceremonies.

Chiffchaff   *Phylloscopus collybita*   11 cm

Breeds in small numbers in mixed deciduous woodland, often in glades and on swamp edges. The song is a jerky ditty based on the two notes in its name – 'chiff, chaff, chaff, chiff . . .' Prefers to breed and feed among older and taller trees than the willow warbler, and usually sings from high among them. The call note 'hweet' is sharper that the willow warbler's and more monosyllabic. The chiffchaff differs from the willow warbler by its – usually – darker legs, somewhat duller hue and its voice. In rare instances, birds of Asian origin (race *tristis*) are seen in western Europe during autumn. They are duller, more brownish grey, without the touch of yellow on throat and breast. Returns in spring a little earlier than the willow warbler.

Garden warbler   *Sylvia borin*   14 cm

The only warbler of the *Sylvia* family to nest above the conifer line. It occurs as far north as the Arctic coast in fertile river valleys and gardens. Its secretive existence and inconspicuous appearance make its song the most distinctive characteristic – a bubbling verse of clear melodious notes. Its other calls are a short 'cherr' and – the warning note – a rhythmically repeated 'tchack'.

Arctic warbler	Willow warbler	Chiffchaff	Garden warbler

Arctic warbler

Willow warbler

Willow warbler

juvenile

Chiffchaff

Garden warbler

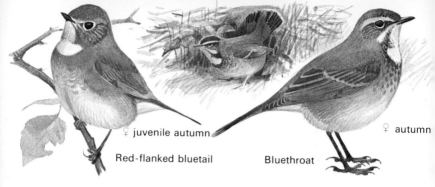

♀ juvenile autumn

Red-flanked bluetail

Bluethroat

♀ autumn

Red-flanked bluetail *Tarsiger cyanurus* 14 cm

Winters in southeast Asia but breeds in deep unspoiled conifer forests in north-eastern Europe where the population depends partly on the weather during the migration period at the end of May. It can be quite common in some years but leads a rather secluded existence and is very shy when singing from midnight until sunrise, mostly from the top of a spruce tree. The loud song has thrush-like short phrases. When agitated there is a short, low-pitched, rather soft 'huit'. Year-old males sing but cannot otherwise be distinguished from females by plumage. Female-coloured birds may be less spectacular, but they still make a special impression with their angular head, oddly 'turned-up-nose' bill and distinct pale eye-ring and bib. The rusty-red flanks are always very prominent, while the bluetail sometimes just looks dark in the half-light of the forest. Insects are its main diet.

Bluethroat *Luscinia svecica* 14 cm

Breeds commonly in flourishing mountain birch forest and waist-high willow thickets, often beside flowing water. Male and female throat markings are variable. Some males have only a little red and blue, while females can have distinct touches of blue, and their base colour is sometimes creamy yellow. Relatively unafraid, but with secretive habits, it usually hops about on the ground under bushes, and has a chat-like habit of jerking its distinctive tail with rust-coloured side patches. The male bird's song varies a great deal in intensity and content. The full-scale performance is an unending burst of bright delicate notes, rapidly trilling and bubbling, often with accelerating bell notes 'tritritritri ...' or 'tingtingting ...' Imitative notes are also interwoven, together with the summoning call, usually 'tsi tchak-tchak ...' Lives on insects, berries and fruit.

Red-flanked bluetail

Bluethroat

Red-flanked bluetail

♂

♀

Bluethroat

♂

♀

juvenile

Wheatear

juvenile

♀

♂

Wheatear *Oenanthe oenanthe* 15 cm

Open mountain or moorland with boulders and gravel slopes provide the wheatear
with a perfect biotope. It is common from the tree line high into the lava region, and
is also distributed throughout the forest belt in suitable terrain. Thus mountain
walkers may come across pairs of wheatears at any time. Towards midsummer they
can be seen bowing and scraping, jerking their distinctive tail (white with a black
outer edge and middle feathers) and emitting short agitated 'shack' notes and an
occasional 'weet'. The male sings in a flappy song flight, bouncing around like a
yo-yo, producing a fast chatter of crunching and creaking notes preceded by a few
'weets'. Feeds on insects and spiders caught on the ground.

Wheatear

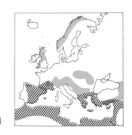

Ring ouzel

juvenile

♀

Ring ouzel

♂

Ring ouzel *Turdus torquatus* 24 cm

Nests relatively sparsely on rocky crags or in gullies on rocky slopes from the upper coniferous zone to the willow zone and, occasionally, at sea-level. Like a blackbird, it often takes to the wing when the passer-by is almost on top of it. On these occasions, and also when it shyly takes refuge behind the crest of a cliff or rock, its wings, paler than those of a blackbird, are a typical feature. When the young are nearby, it usually alights in a low birch tree well away from them and makes a harshly insistent 'teck-teck-teck ...' warning. As with most thrush species, the song is extremely variable, but the basic theme is two or four melancholy piping whistles, sometimes with a brighter, tit-like following note or a twittering tune like the redwing's. When taking to the wing there is a rather dry 'chak'. The female in first winter plumage seldom has much of a pale bar on her breast, which in the males is dingy and indistinct in autumn.

Redwing   *Turdus iliacus*   21 cm

Together with the willow warbler and brambling (and the redpoll in some years),
this is perhaps the most numerous bird of mountain birch forest. It is common
throughout northern Europe, but avoids the densest coniferous forests. The nests,
into the willow zone, and in Iceland in completely treeless areas (with lava blocks),
are often close to human settlement. The song is a rapidly executed, often somewhat
descending tune, 'chirre, cherre, churre, chorre', or a snappier 'ticheu-ticheu'
followed by a rapid, almost hectic twittering. If its nest is nearby it flies around
anxiously in the trees or bushes, jerking one wing to an accompaniment of harshly
clattering 'trrts'. The flight call is a prolonged delicate 'tsuiip' (cf. song thrush).

Song thrush   *Turdus philomelos*   23 cm

In northern Europe occurs mainly in deep and damp coniferous forest, and also in
mountain birch forests. If you flush a small thrush, its identity as a song thrush will
be revealed by a gently ticking 'zip' and, often, by the uniform colour of its upper
parts: the redwing's pale wing contrasts somewhat with its darker back. Also, the
song thrush's under wing coverts are yellowish brown, not russet red. The song,
usually from a tree top, is of pipings and imitative phrases repeated three or four
times. Immatures resemble adults, but with pale spots on the mantle and middle
coverts.

The mistle thrush (*T. viscivorus*) 27 cm breeds in mixed forests with large trees.
It resembles a pale overgrown song thrush with a long white-edged tail. The song is
similar to the blackbird's, although slower and with longer pauses, and it has a
distinctive rattling flight call.

Fieldfare   *Turdus pilaris*   25.5 cm

Common in northern forests, wooded country and parks from sea-level to high into
the mountain birch forest, where it is locally numerous. It usually nests colonially.
Easily recognized in flight by its size, undulating course and white under wing
coverts. The call is a slightly hoarse and rough 'chack-chack-chack (-chackarr)'.
There is also a delicate 'sii' which is primarily heard from migrating flocks in
flight. Its somewhat unmusical song can be passionate, with various cracklings
and bright cracked noises forming a slow verse. It sings from a perch or when
flying between two tree tops.

Redwing

Song thrush

Fieldfare

Redwing

Song thrush

enile

Fieldfare

Siberian tit

winter

summer

Willow tit

Siberian tit   *Parus cinctus*   13 cm

Breeds relatively commonly in northern deep coniferous and mountain birch forests.
It is a large-headed shaggy tit with a long tail, a crown the colour of powdered
chocolate and rusty flanks (which, however, may not be at all prominent towards
summer). The wide repertoire of calls, some resembling those of the willow tit, is a
hoarse 'cheh-cheh-cheh' often preceded by a short 'tsi' or 'tsitsi' and a short 'psit'.
There is also a 'chutt chutt' similar to the crossbill's. An agitated bird emits a
buzzing 'chi-err' and a distinct 'piv piv'. Its song is a slightly hoarse 'chip chiep
chiep chiep chiep' or a short sequence of gently chirping syllables. The Siberian tit
is sedentary and lives on insects, spiders and seeds. During summer it hides a store
of food in cracks in the bark of trees or in lichen overhangs. During winter it often
takes food put out for it, and is bold in the presence of humans.

    The willow tit (*P. montanus*) 11.5 cm breeds commonly in coniferous, mixed and
mountain birch forest, and has the same life-style as the Siberian tit.
Its song is like the wood warbler's, a slowly repeated 'tu-tu-tu-tu-tu'.

Finches *Fringillidae*

All finches have a relatively thick bill appropriate to their seed diet, are gregarious (to a greater or lesser degree) and have an undulating flight. Calls, bill shapes, wing markings (if any) and rump colour are important recognition characteristics. Brambling and redpoll are very common in the mountains and northern forests. Apart from the species described here, the distribution area also includes the chaffinch (*Fringilla coelebs*) which occurs throughout the conifer belt and also appears to have recently expanded its distribution area northwards, and the siskin (*Carduelis spinus*). The siskin is a small finch, rather like the redpoll. The male has highly contrasting green, yellow and black markings, while the female is greyer. The siskin population fluctuates because it lives mainly on spruce seeds, but in some years it is common in the conifer region. The bullfinch (*Pyrrhula pyrrhula*) and crossbill (see parrot crossbill) also occur deep into the mountain birch region.

Buntings *Emberizidae*

Buntings are somewhat similar to finches, but they usually have long tails and more elongated bodies. Most species have a distinctly striated dress, often with contrasting markings. However, there is a great deal of individual variation and considerable differences of dress between different sexes and ages and at different seasons. Song, flight calls and head markings are the best recognition features. Thirteen different species breed in Europe, and apart from those included here, northern Europe also has the yellowhammer (*Emberiza citrinella*) which is common in scrub, forests with glades and on farmland, the ortolan bunting (*E. hortulana*) and the yellow-breasted bunting (*E. aureola*) which occur in open cultivated land with meadows where there are plenty of bushes and close to wetlands. The yellow-breasted bunting inhabits a wide belt stretching from eastern Finland to the east. The striking-looking male has a liver-coloured mantle and crown, and the other parts of his head are black. His bright yellow underparts have a brownish-red bar across the breast, while his wings have a bold white wing bar and narrow white tips to the secondary coverts. The reed bunting (*E. schoeniclus*) is common in or near wetlands, mainly in osiers and willow thickets, throughout northern Europe, and is often found in mountainous birch and willow belts. The male has brownish-red upper parts with thick brownish-black striations, a black head with a white drooping moustache and greyish-white underparts. Its song is a slow chirruping. The female is illustrated on p. 126.

Siberian tit

Willow tit

Redpoll *Acanthis flammea* 13–15 cm

A characteristic bird everywhere in the mountain region, and in more open woodland in the coniferous zone. Numbers vary greatly from year to year. The female is usually dark and dingy in summer, while the male has a bright red front and cap. In winter both sexes are paler with more fawn and brown shades. The redpoll often looks very small flying overhead in deep scoops and emitting a surprisingly loud, metallically bouncing 'dyu, dyu, dyu', or 'dyeck, dyeck, dyeck', with an occasional 'dyuii' (the contact call). Sometimes the flight song is intermingled with a rolling 'turururu' and grasshopper-like buzzings. It will also sing from an exposed branch. Flocks of varying sizes migrate south and west in winter, congregating especially in seed-bearing birch and alder trees. Birch seeds are the staple food.

Arctic redpoll *Acanthis hornemanni* 13.5 cm

Considered by some to be a race of redpoll, the Arctic redpoll is very similar in any case, and sometimes impossible to identify accurately in the field. The unstreaked white rump is the most reliable characteristic, but in many cases there is a striking, paler, 'hoar-frosted' plumage, although there is great variation between individuals. The calls are very much like the redpoll's, but in flight are slower and bounce in slow motion. This bird breeds mainly in tundra with sparse willow and birch vegetation, sometimes overlapping with the redpoll. Occasional individuals mingle with redpoll flocks as far south as central Europe during winter.

Twite *Acanthis flavirostris* 13.5 cm

Breeds relatively commonly in open, wind-swept moorland near the coast and, less commonly, on moorland at higher altitudes inland. In summer it resembles a dark and very earth-bound finch. Its bill is then darker, and the worn white tips of its primaries are not always distinct. On take-off the male's pink upper rump is brilliantly visible, and the birds gyrate in a bobbing flight with bouncy calls, 'chut chululutt'. Their frequent and distinctive call is a nasal and glassily hoarse 'chiut' or 'chway', most often heard from large flocks. After a brief flight they may run about with jerky mouse-like movements, give a short 'chee' and at any time break into a faltering half-chirruping song, not unlike the chatter of a budgerigar. Flocks congregate in winter on coastal marshes, pastures and stubble with plenty of seeds from grasses and wild flowers. The seed diet is augmented by insects in summer.

Twite

Redpoll

Arctic redpoll

juvenile first winter

Redpoll

♀ summer

♂ summer

juvenile first winter

Arctic redpoll

adult

summer

Twite

winter

Brambling *Fringilla montifringilla* 15.5 cm

Breeds very commonly in mountain birch and coniferous forest with occasional softwood trees. The male's distinctive song, a protracted greenfinch-like bleating 'dshweeeh', nasal and monotonous, can be heard everywhere during early summer. Flocks or solitary birds in flight give a distinct 'yeck yeck yeck' and, when settled in a tree, typical broad croaking 'eahps' and 'dshweeehs' their two commonest notes – with a broad 'chway', when migrating. In the breeding grounds they produce many other, often confusing calls. An agitated bird, for example, has a very wide-spaced but regularly ticking 'stitt', and the warning note is a harsh 'aehp'. The male's song may be combined with a rolling 'shrru' like a young thrush which has just left the nest, and there is another version with a rattling trill 'chechechechechecheche', like a speeded-up recording of the redpoll's flight note and somewhat similar to the song of the Arctic warbler. Large flocks of bramblings migrate south as autumn approaches, pausing in fields and on stubble, or visiting beech woods to feed on beechmast. At this time they mingle with other finches and may even visit bird tables. In autumn and winter the contrasting plumage shades are concealed by broad pale feather edges which wear off towards the breeding season so that the beautiful colours emerge. The white rump is a striking feature of the brambling in flight, but is almost entirely lacking in year-old female birds. The food is mainly insects during the nesting season and seeds at other times.

Pine grosbeak *Pinicola enucleator* 20 cm

A rare breeding bird of the conifer belt, preferring swampy spruce woods where there is a scattering of deciduous trees with plenty of bilberry in the undergrowth. During the nesting season pairs may look like two 'lumps' sluggishly hopping about on the ground quite close to the observer, or else doing their Tarzan-the-parrot stunt atop a spruce tree. After munching shoots for about half a minute they will leave the tree top with a few fluttering but beautiful piping 'chulivus' or a simple 'pui'. Then the observer sees heavy, long-tailed finches steering an undulating course for the top of the next spruce. The song is three or four piping arabesques which resemble the contact call but faster, 'chuli chuli chrrui chrrui chui'. They are gregarious in winter, and in some years will migrate south in large numbers. Shoots, buds and berries (mostly rowan in autumn and winter) are the main diet but insects are added in summer.

Brambling

Pine grosbeak

Brambling

Pine grosbeak

Crossbill, juvenile

Two-barred crossbill, juvenile

Parrot crossbill   *Loxia pytyopsittacus*   18 cm

The numbers vary from year to year because it breeds relatively sparsely in coniferous forest. The main diet is pine seeds, unlike the crossbill (*L. curvirostra*) 17 cm, which prefers spruce cones. The parrot crossbill attracts attention with its powerful flight note, a repetitive metallic 'kupp', slightly coarser than the crossbill's but not too easily distinguished from it. Flocks also produce notes of somewhat varying pitch. The song, most frequently heard during winter, is of chattering 'pi-chupps' resembling the call, a somewhat harsh rolling sound, and trills not unlike the greenfinch's. The breeding seasons of the two crossbill species are geared to the ripening of the cones they feed on, with the result that eggs are often laid in February and March. 'Winter' flocks assemble even before the end of spring, and in summer and autumn they lead a vagrant life in search of food. Year-olds can then be distinguished by their brown and greyish-fawn striped dress.

Two-barred crossbill   *Loxia leucoptera*   15 cm

The two-barred crossbill feeds chiefly on larch cones, and its main distribution area is the Siberian taiga where these trees are particularly abundant. When food is scarce birds will irrupt westwards, and some may breed in Scandinavia if there is a good supply of spruce seeds. Recognized by the two bars on its wing, although often only one bar is visible. Its bill is slightly thinner than the crossbill's. The immature is fawn with thick brown streaks and the white wing markings of the adult. Note, however, that immature crossbills may have two narrow but distinct fawn-white wing bars and can be seen all the year round. It has a crossbill-like 'chitt' or 'chett', although weaker, and also a 'puh', a note peculiar to the species, a rather hoarse piping.

Parrot crossbill

Two-barred crossbill

Parrot crossbill

♂

♀

Two-barred crossbill

♀

Rustic bunting *Emberiza rustica* 15 cm

The rustic bunting nests in damp coniferous or mixed forest, often on the borders of swamps where the trees grow thinly. Commoner in the east of our region but scarce in the west. One immediately notes the bright contrasts of the male's white, black and reddish-brown markings. Although not a large bird, in the field the angular head profile, relatively large straight bill and the bold markings on head, breast and flanks give it a bulky appearance. During the autumn and winter these characteristics also serve to distinguish it from other buntings, although it is not easy then to differentiate between the sexes. The song is bright and clear but rather melancholy, variable but roughly 'stuli vuli vuli vulti'. It is somewhat like the hedge sparrow's but may also have a bubbling quality almost resembling the blackcap's. The call is a hard 'tzitt' or 'tsick' like the song thrush's, and when agitated near the nest the rustic bunting gives a long soft 'tsiee' like the penduline tit. It migrates southeast in September and is very rarely seen in western Europe. It lives mainly on various kinds of seeds, but during the nesting season also feeds on insects.

Little bunting *Emberiza pusilla* 13 cm

Nests in sparse waterlogged birch or spruce forests with dwarf birch undergrowth and also in willow areas, frequently close to water. Although occurring rather rarely, it is locally common. It is distinguished from immature and female reed buntings by the bright reddish-brown cheek, crown and – often – throat, the distinct pale eye-ring, the longer, straighter and more pointed bill. Other characteristics that make it different from the reed bunting are the gap between the dark border around its ear coverts (cheek) and bill, and the brown instead of bright brownish-red lesser wing coverts. Its song is somewhat like the rustic bunting's but less coherent and of a rather ticking character, sometimes reminiscent of part of the song of a tree pipit. There may be three or four separate phrases 'titititi-chup chup-sturriep' or 'pie pie-sturi sturi-tulu-chi'. The call is a sharp, metallic 'tsik' or 'tick'. The little bunting lives on seeds and, during the nesting season, insects, especially caterpillars. It migrates southeast in September and October, returning in May, but is a rare visitor in western Europe.

Rustic bunting

Little bunting

Rustic bunting

Little bunting

Lapland bunting *Calcarius lapponicus* 16 cm

Widespread in the mountains and most numerous around the tree line in areas of low bushy vegetation, often near swamps and osiers or beside streams, and on open tundra further north. Often nests in small colonies. A big and rather heavy bunting, the male is easily recognized during the nesting season. The female, too, is relatively distinctive, with well-defined black head markings, fox-red neck and a dark-tipped yellow bill. The thick striations of the upper parts vary considerably in colour. In autumn the male's black markings and red neck under the pale edges are barely discernible. Young females tend to have a touch of brownish yellow over the entire head in autumn. The brownish-red greater coverts, framed by thick whitish wing bars, are a striking characteristic in autumn, particularly in males, which perch in the top of a stunted tree or on a stone. However, when migrating or in winter they hug the ground and move in a fast crouching run. The commonest flight note during migration is a rough grating 'prrrrt', usually preceded or followed by a nasal 'chuh'. Breeding Lapland buntings also use a softer 'djui' and a harder metallic 'schiu'. Birds flying overhead will sometimes give a 'djui' followed, in about two seconds, by 'trui', then repeated, slowly and regularly, in an alternating sequence. The fresh lark-like song, with some resemblance to the bunting's, is from a low perch or in a song flight which is also somewhat like a lark's. The diet is mainly different kinds of seeds, but the young are reared on insects. The migration is to the southeast in September and October.

Snow bunting *Plectrophenax nivalis* 16.5 cm

The white wing markings aid identification in all plumages but they may be limited to traces of dingy white on the secondaries and lesser coverts in some young females. Autumn and winter plumage is mainly ochres and browns. Summer plumage is acquired during the spring as the pale feather edges wear away to reveal the black and white bases of the feathers. Immatures look dull and greyish and their mouse-grey heads and distinct fawn eye-ring remind one of the ortolan bunting. The song is similar to the Lapland bunting's, variable and often simpler, 'tetchutu-tili', or repeated tinkling phrases. The song flight and call are sometimes almost identical to the Lapland bunting's. There is also a bright 'tiu' and a grating 'trrru'. The snow bunting nests in stony terrain well into the lava region, although near the Arctic Ocean it also nests side by side with the Lapland bunting as far as sea-level. The diet is the same as the Lapland bunting's. It reaches its breeding grounds in March and early April and returns to its wintering areas in central and western Europe from October and November.

Lapland bunting

Snow bunting

Lapland bunting

Snow bunting

Little bunting autumn

Reed bunting ♀ autumn

♂ autumn

Rustic bunting

♀ autumn

juvenile
♀
autumn

Lapland bunting

♂ autumn

Snow bunting

♂ winter

♀ winter

♀ juvenile

Ornithological & Conservation Societies in Britain and Ireland

Most counties and some major towns and cities have their own ornithological society: your library should be able to provide the address. Usually these societies hold regular indoor and field meetings – an ideal introduction to the area and the subject – and publish regular reports.

National bodies:

British Trust for Ornithology, Beech Grove, Tring, Herts.
(organize bird ringing, censuses and a wide variety of studies designed for cooperative participation by amateurs. *Bird Study* quarterly, *BTO News* every two months).

Irish Wildbird Conservancy, Royal Irish Academy, 19 Dawson Street, Dublin 2.
(fulfils a similar role in Ireland to the B.T.O.).

Royal Society for the Protection of Birds, The Lodge, Sandy, Beds.
(reserve network available to members, junior branch Young Ornithologists' Club organizes cooperative fieldwork. Colour magazine *Birds* quarterly).

Wildfowl Trust, Slimbridge, Gloucestershire.
(network of wildfowl reserves and collections available, organize winter wildfowl counts. Regular bulletin, *Wildfowl News*, and *Wildfowl*, published annually).

Further Reading

The following selection of books is suggested for you to follow up your interest in birds and their lives. Some deal with identification, some with fieldwork and equipment, and some with biology and ecology. All will prove useful sources of further titles.

Batten, L., Flegg, J., Sorenson, J., Wareing, M., Watson, D. and Wright, D., *Birdwatchers' Year*, T. & A. D. Poyser, 1973.
Brown, L., *British Birds of Prey*, Collins, 1976.

Bruun, B. and Singer, A., *The Hamlyn Guide to the Birds of Britain and Europe*, Hamlyn, 1974.

Cramp, Stanley and Simmons, K. E. L., (eds.), *The Birds of the Western Palaearctic*, Oxford University Press, 1977.

Darling, F. Fraser and Boyd, J. Morton, *The Highlands and Islands*, Collins, 1964.

Fisher, J. and Flegg, J., *Watching Birds*, T. & A. D. Poyser, 1974; Penguin Books, 1978 (in paperback).

Flegg, J., *Discovering Bird Watching*, Shire Publications, 1973.

Flegg, J. J. M., *Binoculars, Cameras and Telescopes*, B.T.O. Field Guide, 1971.

Fry, C. H. and Flegg, J. J. M., *World Atlas of Birds*, Mitchell Beazley, 1974.

Gooders, J., *Where to Watch Birds*, Deutsch, 1967; Pan Books, 1977 (in paperback).

Gooders, J., *Where to Watch Birds in Europe*, Deutsch, 1970; Pan Books, 1977 (in paperback).

Gordon, S., *The Golden Eagle*, Collins, 1955.

Heinzel, H., Fitter, R. and Parslow, J., *The Birds of Britain and Europe*, Collins, 1972.

Hollom, P. A. D., *The Popular Handbook of Rarer British Birds*, H. F. & G. Witherby, 1970.

Lack, D., *Population Studies of Birds*, Oxford University Press, 1966.

Mead, C. J., *Bird Ringing*, B.T.O. Field Guide, 1974.

Moreau, R. E., *The Palaearctic-African Bird Migration System*, Academic Press, 1972.

Nethersole-Thompson, D., *The Greenshank*, Collins, 1951.

Nethersole-Thompson, D., *The Snow Bunting*, Collins, 1966.

Nethersole-Thompson, D., *The Dotterel*, Collins, 1973.

Nethersole-Thompson, D., *Pine Crossbills*, T. & A. D. Poyser, 1973.

Ogilvie, M. A., *Ducks of Britain and Europe*, T. & A. D. Poyser, 1975.

Ogilvie, M. A., *Geese of Britain and Europe*, T. & A. D. Poyser, 1978.

Porter, R. F., Willis, I., Christensen, S. and Nielsen, B. P., *Flight Identification of European Raptors*, T. & A. D. Poyser, 1974.

Rankin, N., *Haunts of British Divers*, Collins, 1947.

Sharrock, J. T. R., (ed.), *The Atlas of Breeding Birds in Britain and Ireland*, B.T.O., 1977.

Thomson, A. L., *A New Dictionary of Birds*, Nelson, 1964.

Voous, K. H., *Atlas of European Birds*, Nelson, 1960.

Watson, D., *Birds of Moor and Mountain*, Oliver and Boyd, 1972.

Welty, J. C., *The Life of Birds*, Saunders, 1975.

Witherby, H. F., Jourdain, F. C. R., Ticehurst, N. F. and Tucker, B. W., *The Handbook of British Birds*, 5 vols, H. F. & G. Witherby, 1938–41.

Index